AUTISM
HANDBOOK
FOR PARENTS

AUTISM
HANDBOOK
FOR PARENTS

*Facts and Strategies
for Parenting Success*

JANICE E. JANZEN

Library of Congress Cataloging-in-Publication Data

Janzen, Janice E.
  Autism handbook for parents : facts and strategies for parenting success / Janice E. Janzen.
      p. cm.
  Previously published as: Autism--facts and strategies for parents. c1999.
  Includes bibliographical references.
  ISBN-13: 978-1-59363-361-5 (pbk.)
  ISBN-10: 1-59363-361-0 (pbk.)
  1. Autism in children--Handbooks, manuals, etc. 2. Parents of autistic children--Handbooks,
manuals, etc. I. Title.
  RJ506.A9J36 2009
  618.92'85882--dc22
                            2008055474

This work and the contents herein are published under a license with Hammill Institute on
Disabilities and is also currently published by Hammill Institute on Disabilities under the
title *Autism Facts and Strategies* © 2006 by Hammill Institute on Disabilities. 8700 Shoal Creek
Boulevard, Austin, Texas, 78757-6897, Tel. (512) 451-3521, Fax. (512) 451-3728, http://www.
hammill-institute.org.

Edited by Jennifer Robins
Cover and Layout Design by Marjorie Parker

ISBN-13: 978-1-59363-361-5
ISBN-10: 1-59363-361-0

Printed in the United States of America.

At the time of this book's publication, all facts and figures cited are the most current available.
All telephone numbers, addresses, and Web site URLs are accurate and active. All publications,
organizations, Web sites, and other resources exist as described in the book, and all have been
verified. The authors and Prufrock Press Inc., make no warranty or guarantee concerning the
information and materials given out by organizations or content found at Web sites, and we
are not responsible for any changes that occur after this book's publication. If you find an error,
please contact Prufrock Press Inc.

Prufrock Press Inc.
P.O. Box 8813
Waco, TX 76714-8813
Phone: (800) 998-2208
Fax: (800) 240-0333
http://www.prufrock.com

CONTENTS

PART I: UNDERSTANDING AUTISM

PART II: TREATMENTS AND SERVICES

PART III: EDUCATIONAL INTERVENTIONS

PART IV: BASIC STRATEGIES

PART V: THE GIFTS

FOREWORD

When my child was diagnosed with autism, it was as if I had found myself at the base of a mountain. Looming before me was a challenge not chosen, but thrust on me by fate. Yet, in order to help my child, there was only one thing to do—start climbing.

Early in my search for help, an autism specialist handed me a batch of papers that explained how best to facilitate learning for children with autism. This writing was so clear and succinct that I sent copies to *everyone* involved in my son's life. As it turned out, Jan Janzen was the author.

Sometimes I find it hard to believe that there are people who would *choose* to climb the mountain in order to help others find their way. Jan Janzen is one of those rare people. She sees autism from the vantage of more than 25 years of teaching experience. We can learn much from her perspective.

The *Autism Handbook for Parents: Facts and Strategies for Parenting Success* is filled with useful information, from the answer to your first question—"What is autism?"—to discussion of the more complicated issues such as choosing treatments and educational programs. It is a resource you will refer to again and again.

This book is not only a carefully drawn map for you, the parent of a child diagnosed with autism, it also is a hand stretched out to steady you and to give you a boost along the way.

Elizabeth King Gerlach
Author, *Autism Treatment Guide*

ACKNOWLEDGMENTS

Over the years, many people have contributed to my knowledge of autism and the contents of this book. Although much of what I have learned came from my numerous colleagues in the field of autism, my most direct teachers were the children themselves and their parents. The parents have shared their concerns, their insights, and their hopes that services will be appropriate and adequate to help their children develop to the greatest of their abilities. To those parents, I wish to say thank you, and I hope that my work has made a difference. My appreciation to all for helping me grow.

I want to acknowledge the help of several parents who have had a direct influence on the contents of this book. Specifically, three parents contributed their time and experience to ensure that the contents were both accurate and useful. Elizabeth King Gerlach, author of *Autism Treatment Guide* and owner of Four Leaf Press in Eugene, OR, read most of the book twice and provided valuable feedback. She also allowed us to include her son's poem, "I Hear the Beat" (see pp. 189–190). Wayne Jasper, the director of Parents Helping Parents, a parent advocacy center in Santa Clara, CA, reviewed some of the material for accuracy and provided some important insights. Valerie Rynne, a parent advocate who lives in Menlo Park, CA, read the first draft of the book and parts of the final draft. It was Valerie's useful comments that made this book longer, more accurate, and I believe more useful.

I also want to thank the parents who shared stories and thoughts about their child's autism and gave permission to include the artwork and poetry in the final chapter. Bill Seaton, a father from McMinneville, OR, shared his very personal feelings about his relationship with his adult son, Burleigh. Bill allowed me to include the haiku (see p. 185) that expresses his insights so clearly.

Eileen and John Miller of Roseburg, OR, gave me permission to include the drawings on pages 187–188, produced by their daughter, Kim. Not only did they share stories about Kim's life, but Eileen provided the story of their struggles to protect Kim's safety (see pp. 123–125). Another mother, Karen Williams of Washington, PA, shared her daughter's drawings (see p. 186). Karen provided stories to illustrate how Rosemarie's drawings contributed to her development.

I want to thank Margaret Eastham of Ottawa, Ontario, Canada, for giving me permission to include her son David's poetry in both of my books. Over the years, David's wonderfully insightful poetry has given me a deeper understanding of the nature of autism. I believe it will affect you in the same way (see p. 191).

My thanks and appreciation also go to Ricky Bourque, the editor of both of my books, who seems to have become part of my family.

Finally, thanks to Marvin, my husband and most trusted supporter, who read it all many times and put up with my work as we traveled from coast to coast in our RV. Without his enthusiastic support and that of our four children, I would never have had a career.

INTRODUCTION

This book is written especially for you, the parent who has just discovered that your child has autism. You probably feel that you are groping around in a world gone a bit crazy—nothing is quite the same as it was before. Although it is a relief to know there is a name for your child's problems and there are people out there who understand how to help, you probably have many questions and concerns, and don't quite know how to proceed.

I have worked closely with many families in your position. I know how confusing it is to work with professionals who seem to talk in another language, and to find that many books and articles about autism are either reports of research or stories about individuals with autism who have little in common with your child. It also is unsettling to find out that there are many contradictory ideas about autism and what should be done.

I hope this book will provide a starting place and some direction to your journey. It contains some basic information to help you understand:

1. your child's diagnosis,
2. the effects of autism on learning and behavior,
3. your role as an advocate,
4. the important first decisions you must make for your child's future,
5. how to prevent and manage many of your child's problems, and
6. how to teach your child some critical early skills.

When you understand *why* your child does the things he does, you have a basis for making day-to-day decisions that match your child's real needs. You will be able to provide the support he needs to prevent many behavior problems. You also will be able to communicate that information to teachers and others who are involved with your child's program, to make transitions less stressful and to save precious teaching time.

This book is just a beginning. You will need considerable more information to be truly effective as an advocate, teacher, and parent for your child. In order to keep this book small and quick to read, I have included several references for more information, including my first book, *Understanding the Nature of Autism: A Practical Guide*. That book is a comprehensive and easy-to-read manual written for parents, teachers, and other professionals. It contains a broad range of in-depth and practical information to help you implement the main strategies. There also are examples of real situations to clarify the basic points.

Both this book and *Understanding the Nature of Autism* are written from the perspective of more than 25 years of experience in learning about autism, teaching those who have autism, and working with their families and teachers. My career in autism has provided me with many wonderful opportunities to learn more about autism. It has been challenging, but incredibly rewarding—the most creative work I could imagine.

As you read the book, please keep the following in mind:

- I have used the masculine pronouns (he, him, his) throughout his book because approximately 80% of those with autism are boys. The content, of course, also applies to girls with autism even though the feminine pronoun isn't used.

- In most cases, I tried to avoid using professional jargon so the text would be easier to read and understand. Some commonly used terms were included in the glossary because you will encounter them as you continue your study of autism and as you work with your child's service providers.

- I always use the term *autism* rather than the term *autistic*. Most of my colleagues and I prefer to focus on the person first, and then on the disability. I include phrases such as *child with autism*, *those with autism*, *autism services*, and *autism spectrum*. The only time you will see the other term in this book is when it is used to reference the label in the

American Psychiatric Association's *Diagnostic and Statistical Manual* (*DSM-IV–TR*), or when it is the given name of a model program or in the title of a published article or book.

◆ Because I am a teacher, the major thrust of this book is to provide information about appropriate educational services and strategies, how to evaluate educational and other services, and how to obtain appropriate services for your child.

PART I
UNDERSTANDING AUTISM

FACTS ABOUT AUTISM

IN THE BEGINNING

When you first saw your baby, he looked like sweet perfection. You had many hopes and dreams for the special things he would do and the experiences you would share. For a while, all seemed well as you got to know each other. But, as time went by, you began to have some nagging feelings that something might not be quite right. Perhaps a neighbor or grandparent commented that your child was developing differently. If you have other children, you may have noticed that this child wasn't doing some of the things his brother or sister did at the same age. Your baby didn't:

- begin to look at you with flirty eyes;
- watch you and begin to coo and wait for you to take your turn cooing, then imitate you and keep the turn-taking game going;
- look at you, then to another object, and back to you, as if trying to get you to share attention with something else;
- verbalize to get your attention, point to a dropped toy, and look between you and the toy so you would pick it up;
- watch people and follow their movements, and look from one to the other as if following their conversations; and
- cuddle or snuggle into your body as other babies do. One mother said that she could never comfort her child. Whenever she picked him up, he became more tense and rigid and screamed even louder.

Failure to develop these early communication and interaction skills is the first, most common symptom of autism that a well-trained and alert pediatrician recognizes in babies between 12 and 30 months of age. In other families, the scenario is somewhat different.

In some cases, a child appears to develop normally, then begins to lose the early communication and interaction skills or fails to develop more advanced language and social skills. In these cases, the indicators of autism are most clear and apparent between 2 and 3 years of age.

In other situations, some more capable and quite verbal young children show few, or only mild, characteristics until they are 8 to 10 years of age, when time pressures and the demand for higher level thinking and social judgment make the indicators more obvious.

WHAT PARENTS NEED TO KNOW

Parents need to know the real problem as early as possible so they can get the help their child needs, because intensive and appropriate early intervention is indeed critical. Some parents are lucky to have a pediatrician who understands autism, recognizes the early symptoms, and refers them to the appropriate services and support. Other families are not so fortunate. They may have searched for a diagnosis and help for some time and were told to relax and that their child would develop in his own time. Sometimes children with the symptoms of autism are given other diagnoses. When their parents see that their child is different from the other children with that same diagnosis, they continue to search for a diagnosis that truly matches their child's symptoms.

THE SEARCH FOR INFORMATION BEGINS

Now that your child's problems have been diagnosed, you begin a new search to answer your questions, find out how to help your child, and deal with your own feelings and emotions. At this stressful time, it is easy to become overloaded with information, much of it contradictory.

Another problem at this stage is the confusing number of labels that in some way relate to autism—so many labels, in fact, that parents may begin to distrust their child's diagnosis. Now you have a million questions. Exactly what is autism? What causes autism? What do all of those different labels mean?

A GENERAL DEFINITION OF AUTISM

Autism is a neurobiological disorder of development that causes discrepancies or differences in the way the brain processes information. This information-processing difference affects the ability to:

- understand and use language to interact and communicate with people;
- understand and relate in typical ways to people, events, and objects in the environment;
- understand and respond in typical ways to sensory stimuli (e.g., pain, hearing, taste); and
- learn and think in the same way as normally developing children.

These learning and thinking differences cause confusion, frustration, and anxiety that is expressed in a variety of unexpected ways that include withdrawing, engaging in unusual repetitive behaviors, and—occasionally in extreme cases or situations—by aggression or self-injury. Although the learning and thinking style found in autism is unique, it is predictable and different from the problems caused by other development disabilities.

At this time, there are no medical or psychological tests to diagnose autism. Rather, the diagnosis is based on the presence of a cluster of behavioral systems (see Figure 1).

UNRAVELING THE LABELING MAZE

Autism was first defined by Dr. Leo Kanner of Johns Hopkins Medical Center in 1943. When compared to other developmental disabilities such as blindness, deafness, and retardation, autism is a relatively new condition; as such, there are still no definitive answers to some of our questions.

Kanner's definition of autism was based on a description of only 11 children with very similar symptoms; thus, it was believed that only a few children had autism and that they were all very much alike. The terms *classic autism*, *early infantile autism*, *childhood autism*, or *Kanner's syndrome* were the first labels used for this limited number of children. As we have learned more about autism over the years, a number of different labels have been used to identify this population of children.

Autism Spectrum Disorders

After more than 60 years of study, it is clear that there is more than one type or degree of autism—there is an autism spectrum. This means that the effects of autism can range from mild to severe, that the intellectual ability of those with autism can range from gifted to severely intellectually impaired, and that autism can co-occur with many other conditions and syndromes, such as retardation, hearing and vision impairments, cerebral palsy, Down syndrome, and seizure disorders.

Although all persons with autism share common types of symptoms and a common style of learning and thinking, each individual is unique because the severity and pattern of his autism and intellectual ability are unique. Each child has lived and learned from unique experiences, and each child's interests, fears, likes, and dislikes are different.

No single behavior is indicative of autism, nor will any child show all of the behaviors listed. It is the pattern of indicators from each category that is significant. Some indicators may be intense, others more mild.

Language/Communication
- Facial expressions are flat or limited
- Rarely or never uses gestures
- Rarely initiates communication
- Fails to imitate actions or sounds
- Uses little or no speech or is overly verbal
- Repeats or echoes words and phrases
- Uses unusual vocal intonation/rhythm
- Seems not to understand word meanings
- Understands and uses words literally

Relating
To people:
- Is unresponsive
- Has no social smile
- Does not communicate with eyes
- Eye contact is limited and fleeting
- Seems content when left alone
- Seeks social contact in unusual ways
- Does not play turn-taking games
- Uses adult's hand as a tool

To the environment:
- Play is repetitive
- Is upset by or resists changes
- Develops rigid routines
- Drifts about aimlessly
- Exhibits intense and obsessive interests

Responses to Sensory Stimuli
- Sometimes seems deaf
- Is oversensitive to sound
- Exhibits panic related to specific sounds
- Plays with light and reflections
- Flicks fingers before eyes
- Pulls away when touched
- Strongly avoids certain clothes, foods
- Is attracted to patterns, textures, odors
- Is very inactive or very active
- Whirls, spins, bangs head, or bites wrist
- Jumps up and down, flapping hands
- Exhibits unusual or no response to pain

Developmental Discrepancies
Skills are either very good or very delayed, and the child learns skills out of the normal sequence. For example:
- Reads, but does not understand meaning
- Draws detailed pictures, but cannot button coat
- Is very good with puzzles and pegs, but is very poor at following directions
- Walks at a normal age, but cannot communicate
- Has clear echoed speech, but self-initiated speech is labored
- Can do things sometimes, but not at other times

FIGURE 1. Summary of behavioral indicators of autism in young children.

Pervasive Developmental Disorders

In an effort to learn more about the causes and potential treatments for children with autism spectrum disorders, researchers are trying to sort these children into subgroups with very similar characteristics. The classification system currently in use was developed by the American Psychiatric Association (APA) and was published in its text revision of the fourth edition of the *Diagnostic and Statistical Manual* (*DSM-IV–TR*). In that book, the various subgroups are listed under the general heading of Pervasive Developmental Disorders (PDD).

PDD is a synonym for autism spectrum disorders. It is used in the *DSM-IV–TR* to describe a condition that impacts or pervades all parts of development to some degree. It implies that development is not simply delayed, as in retardation, but distorted or different. A diagnosis of PDD indicates the presence of autism *or* a closely related neurobiological disorder. The subgroups included under the general category of PDD are:

- *Autistic Disorder*. This typical form of autism shows major delays and distortions in development by the age of 2 years. The behavioral symptoms cluster in four areas, as shown in Figure 1.
- *Pervasive Developmental Disorder–Not Otherwise Specified (PDD–NOS) or Atypical Autism*. This term is used for those who have most of the symptoms of autism, but not all, or some of the symptoms are very mild or not clear. PDD–NOS also is used for those who once had the complete symptom cluster, but some symptoms are no longer apparent.
- *Asperger's Disorder, more commonly known as Asperger's syndrome (AS)*. This term is used to describe children who have many of the symptoms of autism, but have intellectual abilities near or within the normal range. Although their verbal abilities initially develop rather normally, the problems relate to understanding and using the language in typical ways, understanding the perspective of others, and managing social situations. These children also have intense, overly focused interests and repetitive behavior. The deficits of those

with Asperger's syndrome are less obvious, but the discrepancies are greater (e.g., sometimes their strengths mask the severity of the language and social perception problems). It is not yet clear whether AS is a separate syndrome, or if it is simply a high-functioning form of autism. Many individuals who later receive this diagnosis had the typical symptoms of autism as very young children. Other terms have been used to describe this group including *high-functioning autism (HF)*, *more able*, *nearly normal*, and *mildly autistic*.

◆ *Rett's syndrome and childhood disintegrative disorder.* These are labels of conditions that begin after a period of normal development, followed by severe disintegration of skills and abilities while the symptoms of autism develop. Rett's syndrome generally affects girls, and childhood disintegrative disorder primarily affects boys.

Some parents are told that their child has an *autistic-like condition*. This term was used by many professionals during a time in which:

◆ little was known about autism and there was no clear definition,

◆ autism was thought to be caused by parental rejection,

◆ autism was seen as a hopeless condition, and

◆ a diagnosis of autism was seen as a stigma.

As more and more is learned about autism, the stigma has virtually disappeared, and the term *autistic-like* rarely is used. Dr. Edward Ritvo, an expert in autism, has said that being autistic-like would be similar to being pregnant-like; if the symptoms are present, the condition is present.

Perhaps the most important thing to remember is that Pervasive Development Disorders is a synonym for autism spectrum disorders, and that the subgroups of PDD simply refer to a form or variation of autism.

The labels that were commonly used in the past are included here to help you interpret information written prior to 1994. The *DSM* is revised periodically to reflect new information. Each revision has included different terminology or labels. The *DSM-IV–TR* diagnostic criteria are too long, detailed, and technical to include in this book. If you wish to see the *DSM-IV–TR*, you can get a copy at your local library, or ask the person who made your child's diagnosis to explain the criteria to you.

For a discussion on the implications of the various diagnostic labels on eligibility for special services, see pages 62–63.

CAUSES OF AUTISM

Autism is a *syndrome*, or condition, with many possible causes. Anything that makes the central nervous system develop abnormally, either before or after birth, can cause autism. In most cases, the event that initially triggers these developmental differences probably occurred during the early period of fetal development. In some cases, the trauma that causes autism may have occurred during birth or even after birth.

Although it is not always possible to identify the exact cause of the damage, several conditions have been implicated (see Figure 2). It is important to know that contrary to earlier beliefs, autism and other neurobiological disorders are *not* caused by vaccinations, parental rejection, lack of love, or inadequate parenting skills.

Knowing the cause is important for medical research and it helps parents get appropriate genetic and medical information. However, appropriate education and treatment is not dependent on knowing the cause of autism. Rather, effective education and intervention is based on an understanding of the learning style common to this group of individuals.

INCIDENCE OF AUTISM

Autism always has been considered a low-incidence condition, but it is not as rare as once believed. Prior to 1990, the incidence was thought to be one in 2,500 births. Now there is evidence that the incidence of

Viral Infections
Such as congenital rubella, cytomegalovirus, herpes simplex virus infection

Metabolic Imbalances
Such as thyroid disease and phenylketonuria

Exposure to Alcohol and Drugs
Such as in cocaine-addicted babies and those with fetal alcohol syndrome

Exposure to Environmental Chemicals
Such as lead and other toxic chemicals

Genetic–Chromosomal Factors
Some families have more than one child with autism or other developmental disabilities. Fragile X and Down syndrome, both genetic disorders, commonly co-occur with autism.

Oxygen Deprivation or Overexposure During or Shortly After Birth
As in retinopathy of prematurity

After Severe Viral Infections and Traumatic Brain Injury
As in encephalitis, spinal meningitis, or brain injury from a fall or severe car accident. In these situations, symptoms of autism will occur after the normal age of onset.

FIGURE 2. Some of the conditions implicated as causes of autism.

autism is reaching higher proportions. It has been reported that as many as 1 in 150 people are now diagnosed with autism (Boutot, 2009b).

These newer statistics are a result of several factors. First, we know more about autism and are better at identifying the various ways that autism presents itself. Pediatricians and psychologists now are more aware of the autism symptoms and the importance of early intervention. Another explanation for the increasing incidence is that most professionals no longer avoid giving a diagnosis of autism now that there is no stigma attached to the label.

Although these factors make a significant difference in the number of children diagnosed with autism, they cannot account for the near-epidemic increases in the condition (Rimland, 1995). Some of the suspected factors in this monumental increase involve environmental drugs, pollutants, and perhaps vaccinations. We know that the incidence of autism in fetal alcohol syndrome and in drug-affected babies is significantly high. We also know of clusters of cases that occurred downwind of a site where waste products from a plastics plant were dumped. One early study showed that a significant number of children with autism had parents working in chemical industries before and/or during pregnancy. It has been speculated that the increasing incidence might be related to vaccines, including the measles-mumps-rubella (MMR) vaccine. However, many studies indicate that there is little evidence to this belief (Tincani & Groeling, 2009).

Research continues in the quest to answer the critical questions about autism—its causes, incidence, the differences in brain development, and the potential cures or preventions.

VALUE OF ACCURATE DIAGNOSTIC LABELS

Some professionals suspect that autism is being overdiagnosed—as if autism were the "diagnosis of the year"; but those close to the field know that the increasing incidence is indeed real. And, while many professionals feel that labels are unimportant or even stigmatizing, the use of correct labels is critical, especially in autism, because labels convey information to ensure appropriate treatment, education, and support. Until teachers and parents have the correct information, they will not know how to assess and address the child's needs adequately. When we have stomach pains, we first believe it is a symptom of indigestion or the flu, and we avoid seeking a medical treatment. If the pain continues, we finally see a doctor, who begins to ask questions and takes a variety of tests to determine the exact cause of the pain. Treatment provided before the exact source of the pain is identified either could have no effect or could seriously complicate the problem. And so it is with autism.

Accurate diagnoses and the use of clear labels are critically important to families for many other reasons:

* to obtain accurate genetic counseling;
* to be alert for symptoms of medical problems that commonly occur in autism;
* to obtain appropriate medical treatment (e.g., those with autism respond differently to certain drugs, often requiring lower than the recommended dosages); and
* to ensure that educational and other services match the specific needs of those with autism through the life span. In fact, special education law includes autism as one of the conditions that schools must identify in order to provide appropriate educational services.

One mother complained that her child was having many behavior problems and making almost no progress in her school program, and the teachers didn't seem to know what to do. Once it was discovered that her daughter had autism, the mother and the teachers could begin to understand the child's situation. As they worked together to provide an appropriate program, the child began to make quite amazing progress.

Diagnostic labels provide access to information, support systems, and appropriate services over the life span. Autism has lost much of its stigma now that we know it is not caused by rejecting parents, and with an understanding of the neurobiological nature of the learning and behavior problems, we have more effective intervention strategies. Now that society is more tolerant of diversity, perhaps people can understand and accept unfamiliar or unexpected behavior and allow these children to live a more rewarding life in the community.

Most parents are sad, but relieved, to know that someone understands their child's problems and knows how to proceed. One mother, Mary Anne Seaton, said that her son's diagnosis was "the beginning of turning my life around and setting the direction for my son and our family. Having the opportunity to learn how my son's disability affects him clearly changed our lives. Without that information, we would not have survived."

You may feel unsure about the accuracy of your child's diagnosis. If you still wonder whether your child truly has autism after reading this chapter, it would be reasonable to have him reevaluated at another evaluation center. If two evaluations lead to a diagnosis of autism, there is little need to seek another opinion. One of the pioneers in the study of autism, Dr. Lorna Wing, who has a daughter with autism, has said that if anyone suspects autism, it is probably true, for if the symptoms were not present, autism would never be suspected.

TREATMENTS OR CURES

As you begin to gather information and deal with autism, your first concern is likely to relate to treatments and cures. The answer to this concern is the same as it was almost 20 years ago, when Frith (1989) reported, "At this time there are no medical or behavioral treatments that cure autism, and it is highly unlikely that anything will be found in the near future that can totally reverse the effects of a developmental process of this magnitude" (p. 15).

Even though there are no cures for autism, there are numerous treatments (see Chapter 4). A highly structured educational program that addresses the predictable deficits of autism is currently the only treatment that shows positive, long-term effects and holds promise for every child with autism. The earlier this intervention begins, the more likely that a child will reach his or her potential.

POTENTIAL FOR THOSE WITH AUTISM

It is very difficult to determine the potential of any young child, especially one with autism. So much depends on the interactive effects of the degree of the autism, the child's native intellectual ability, co-occurring disabilities, life experiences, and the type of support received. Some children who were severely affected by autism at age 3 make great gains and can function at a higher level when older. Others who seemed more mildly affected at age 3 show more severe effects after the age of 9 or so, when analytic and creative thinking and subtle social skills and judgments are required. Although those with autism are vulnerable during adolescence and adulthood, we know that with individualized support systems to compensate for the deficits common to those with autism, most can live productive and satisfying lives in the community as adults. Some will require a personal assistance; others can succeed with less support.

Some adults with autism live with their own or foster families, while others live in group homes or alone in their own homes with periodic assistance. Some adults with autism graduate from high school, and a few get advanced college degrees and have successful careers in highly specialized fields of interest. A few individuals do marry. Those with autism are employed with varying levels of support in hospitals, post offices, warehouses, libraries, banks, high-tech industries, landscape and nursery businesses, and most other businesses in which accuracy and attention to detail are valued more than the need for speed and ability to make judgments and decisions.

UNDERSTANDING THE EFFECTS OF AUTISM

2

I met my first student with autism in Alaska in 1972 while teaching a class of young children with communication disorders. At that time, I had no special education training. Needless to say, I was confused by this child's behavior and I made many mistakes, often making the problems worse. That child challenged me to read and learn about autism.

UNDERSTANDING THE CHILD'S PERSPECTIVE

One of the first things I was lucky enough to read was a small piece written by Wing (1980), in which she said, "An autistic child can be helped only if a serious attempt is made to see the world from his point of view, so that the adaptive function of much of his peculiar behavior can be understood in the context of his handicaps" (p. xi).

Since that time, the focus of my work has been to understand the perspective of people with autism. How do they see the world? How do they process information? I discovered that if we understand their perspective, we can figure out why they do the things they do and what is likely to help. Without an understanding of the child's perspective, we are likely to misinterpret his signs of confusion, frustration, and anxiety, instead perceiving them as deliberate noncompliance, defiance, belligerence, or aggression. These misperceptions are based on the point of view we developed from experiences with typically developing children. Interventions based on these misperceptions are likely to increase the child's confusion, frustration, and anxiety, and will make things worse—or, at best, will not help the situation.

Here are a few examples of misinterpreting the cause or meaning of a child's behavior:

- When a child does not respond to our directions, we often believe he is being deliberately noncompliant, defiant, or belligerent. However, children with autism generally will do what they are told if they completely understand what to do. In fact, they will do exactly what they are told, in exactly the way we tell them to do it. One frustrated mother complained, "No matter what I do, Tony never does what I tell him to do." During my first visit to their home, I discovered that he did do *everything* she asked, but he did it for such a short time that his busy mother never saw him do it. For example, she was at the stove finishing dinner preparations when she said, "Dinner is ready. Go to the table." While she was still occupied, Tony drifted quietly to the table, stood a moment, and then wandered off. But, he did exactly what she told him to do—"Go to the table." Tony was compliant; the problem was that he did not know what to do when he got to the table, nor did he know that he was to wait for his mom to bring dinner. Therefore, we had a teaching problem, rather than a problem of noncompliance.

- Often, a lack of response is seen as a lack of ability when it might be a lack of motivation. Most children with autism see no reason to do a boring or meaningless task just because someone says to do it. They do not understand or value doing something simply to please another person. As a part of my initial autism training, one of the training staff was coaching me as I worked one-on-one with a 4-year-old boy. I had just placed three picture cards on the table and asked the child to give me the picture of the truck. He continued to sit back in his chair and look at the pictures, but made no response. After repeating the request with still no response, I removed one card to make it easier. Still he did not respond. As I started to remove another card, my coach told me to spread all of the cards out on the table. When I asked again for the truck, the child sat up, surveyed the array of cards, and quickly handed me the correct one. I discovered that a task that does not match the child's ability level—be it either too easy or too hard—is definitely not motivating. I also learned that before working with a child, one must know as much as possible about that child, and not presume that a lack of response is a lack of ability.

◆ Occasionally, a child's lack of response is seen as noncompliance or defiance when, in fact, the child is unable to produce the required response. Terri was truly nonverbal at age 7 when she entered school. She made considerable progress during the first few weeks of school: She learned to sit and work during one-to-one (1:1) sessions, she could follow many directions quickly and imitate motor movements, and had many other skills. However, she could never imitate a verbal response. When relaxing in quiet solitary play, she would hum and make little chirping sounds, but whenever she was asked to imitate even her own sounds, she would give eye contact, look very intent, and move her lips—but nothing came out. In fact, on several occasions, she tried so hard that a few tears rolled down her cheeks.

The key to understanding your child's perspective is to understand how he learns, how he thinks, and how he processes information. We know that there is a neurologically based difference in the way those with autism process information. The differences account for most of the problems of learning and behavior for these children.

INFORMATION PROCESSING IN AUTISM

Analytic Processing

First, let's examine the way most people process new information. When we encounter something new, we are alert and a bit tense as we observe and analyze the situation to see how it relates to other things we know. As we begin to make sense of it, we start to relax and give it a label before filing it away until we get more information. We analyze and integrate bits and pieces of new information with bits and pieces of old information and file it away with meaningful labels. Finally, with enough information, the pieces fall together, we get the whole idea, and we say, "Ah-ha! Now I understand." This is an *analytic mode* of processing. All of this happens so quickly and automatically that we do not even think about it unless something goes wrong.

Gestalt Processing

However, the basic information-processing style (variously called *cognitive style* or *learning style*) common to those with autism is not analytic. When they encounter something new, all of the details of the situation are taken in as a chunk and stored quickly without analysis for meaning. This processing style has been called *holistic* or *gestalt processing*.

Just think what this means. Things that occur closely together in time are "chunked" and recorded together. Individual bits and pieces of an event can be recorded separately (like snapshots), or a total event can be recorded as a long routine (like a videotape). A recorded chunk is likely to include the important information that is relevant to the situation as well as the background noise and unrelated pieces of stimuli—all stored together without analysis and any meaningful label.

Let's assume that you are standing in front of the kitchen stove frying bacon while telling your child how to do something. The child's recorded "tape" from this situation could include the shiny switches and dials of the stove; the clothes you are wearing; the rings on your hands; the sounds of the exhaust fan and the sizzling, spattering bacon; noises from the nearby freeway and the TV in the family room; the bird that happened to fly by the window at that moment; the smell of bacon frying; and the fragrance of your hair spray. Everything that occurs within the range of the child's sense at that time is record in his long-term memory without being sorted or analyzed. To the child with autism, the irrelevant information is just as significant as the words you say.

Other Processing Differences

This gestalt (holistic) processing style is a major factor in what is learned and how it is interpreted and understood. Research has shown a number of other associated elements or processing differences that further complicate the picture for those with autism. The differences that most obviously impact learning and behavior relate to the ability to modulate incoming information, to remember information, to manipulate information flexibly, and to process auditory and visual information.

Modulating Sensory Input. Our own sensory system appears to have automatic controls that regulate and modulate the incoming stimulation. We can shut out the background clutter and focus only on the critical events—at least, for a time. When the lights, noises, and stimulation from the environment begin to overwhelm typically developing infants, the babies tuck their fists under their chins, close their eyes, and go to sleep. Their sensory systems virtually turn off for a time.

The sensory systems of those with autism, however, perform inconsistently, so that the information taken in or received from the environment is distorted in some ways. Sometimes the system fluctuates randomly so that the stimulation is received at either too high or too low of a level. Sometimes a child will be overwhelmed with painful stimulation, and at other times the stimulation barely registers. Therefore, the child's behavior and ability to learn will vary considerably from time to time.

One man with autism reported that he knew when something was coming in, but he couldn't tell if it was something he heard or something he saw. Temple Grandin, a woman with autism, is a university professor with a doctoral degree in animal psychology. She has studied and written extensively about autism. She reported that since childhood, her ears were like an open microphone, with every sound magnified and frequently causing pain. She also recalled that the feel of the lace on the slips she had to wear as a child was so overwhelming that she could not focus on anything else.

We see the results of this overstimulation in many children with autism who cover their ears or eyes, run away, and crawl under or behind the furniture in an effort to cut out the stimulation and protect themselves. Stimulation that most people rarely notice can overpower those with autism and lead to tantrums and other unexpected behaviors.

Long-Term Memory for Facts, Routines, and Concrete Information. Remember that an element of gestalt processing is to quickly take in and store chunks of information. This quick storage and firm memory can cause major problems. If the information has not been analyzed for meaning, the incorrect meaning is likely to be attached and remembered forever. Because the information is not analyzed for relevance, the clutter also is remembered forever. One young man became very anxious because he was afraid that his brain would get too full and he might forget something. But, this amazing memory can be a significant strength if information is clarified and presented in meaning ways. There will be more about this challenge discussed in Chapters 9 and 10.

Inflexibility. Those with autism have great difficulty relating and integrating ideas, modifying ideas or rules to accommodate new information, and generalizing new skills and rules to different situations and settings. Without intervention, those with autism will learn and do things exactly as taught, without any variations.

Another aspect of rigidity and inflexibility relates to repetitive thinking and behavior. It is not unusual for a child to get stuck; that is, to perseverate or repeat thoughts, words, conversations, and motor movements over and over as if unable to stop. One 4-year-old would move his foot to step through a doorway, then get stuck and rock back and forth, seemingly unable to take that next step to move on through the door.

Auditory Processing Deficits. In general, we give information, directions, and corrections verbally. Most, but not all, children with autism can hear and remember the things they hear. However, at least two problems interfere with auditory processing and impact learning and behavior:

- These children have difficulty maintaining attention on verbal information. Their attention fades in and out as it is diverted or overwhelmed by background noises. Consequently, there are gaps or missing pieces of information with no trace. The child does not know he missed some information, and we do not know that the information was not received.

- It takes a long time for these children to process, understand, and organize information that they hear and to generate a verbal or motor response. Sometimes this delay is as long as 30 to 45 seconds. Not many of us can wait 30 seconds for some indication that the child is going to do what we asked. Within 10 seconds, we generally repeat the request. Within another 10 seconds, we have used different words in an attempt to clarify the direction. Perhaps we have repeated it again with a raised voice paired with a comment to pay attention. Each time we repeat the direction or change the words, the child has something new to process.

Unlike us, the child cannot process those additional words quickly and realize that we are simply repeating the same information in a different way. Instead the child believes that each statement is different—something new to figure out. Thus, the child becomes overwhelmed by too many meaningless words. If we persist and keep pushing, the child is likely to fall apart into a major tantrum. This is often the cause of tantrums "for no apparent reason." These delayed responses are sometimes perceived as deliberate noncompliance.

Visual Processing Strengths. For children with autism, visual information tends to be easier and faster to process than verbal information. We know that many children with autism are very good at putting together puzzles and sorting things. In fact, some children with autism have photographic memories. Many can learn to read and spell without formal instruction, although they are not likely to attach meaning to the words until they are taught specifically.

We have learned to capitalize on this visual processing strength to compensate for the other processing deficits. When presented with information that is organized visually to clarify the critical elements and relationships, those with autism can be taught to use concepts and skills meaningfully and become more independent. Information provided visually compensates for the auditory problems because it is permanent and always available for later reference.

Although any one of these processing differences would have a significant impact on any child, the combined effects of these differences are magnified many times, impacting every thing and every experience encountered.

EFFECTS OF PROCESSING DIFFERENCES

Although the gestalt processing style is common to all with autism spectrum disorders, the effects will vary in each child depending on the severity of the child's autism, inherent intellectual abilities, life experiences, and interests. Note that I use the word *unable* or *inability* to indicate that these children do not automatically learn to do these things. But, it is important to understand that they can be taught to do or compensate for these problems in some way or to some degree. In general, however, you can expect your young child with autism to exhibit the following traits.

- The child will have difficulty scanning a room or area, selecting and focusing on the relevant or important information, and ignoring the clutter. Rather, those with autism are distracted by the amazing amounts of stimulation in an area at any given time—movements, light, odors, textures, feelings, and sounds. Without the ability to analyze and sort information meaningfully, either everything will have equal importance to the child, or the importance is determined by the child's sensitivities and interests. The wood grain on the wall paneling may be more important than your words, or your child may be more caught up in the reflections in your eyes or your eyelashes than in connecting with your eyes. The child may focus intently on some small detail in the background of a photograph and thus miss the critical focal point for meaning.

- The child will have difficulty processing new and novel information (stimuli). New information increases anxiety and overloads the system. This can explain the difficulty these children have in new situations, their reluctance to try new experiences, and their anxiety when things change. It appears that the range of tolerable stimulation is very narrow for those with autism; they need just enough stimulation to keep them alert, but not so much stimulation that their systems shut down.

- Those with autism learn routines quickly. If a person with autism does something in the same way two times in a row, it tends to become a routine. Without intervention, the routines are likely to include unexpected or irrelevant steps and be stored with little or no practical meaning or purpose. The routine becomes simply what one does in a particular setting or context. Once the routine is in memory, those with autism are compelled to repeat the routine under similar conditions. If we capitalize on this ability, we can incorporate many concepts and skills within the context of everyday, practical routines and help these children to become more independent.

♦ Those with autism have difficulty retrieving information, especially verbal information, in the appropriate sequences. This problem affects their ability to integrate information from past experiences with information from new experiences, to learn cause/effect relationships, to predict future events from past experiences, and to adapt and apply the information to different situations. This also leads to an inability to follow a sequence of directions in the correct order.

♦ They perceive a stream of words—a sentence, phrase, or song—as a single word or chunk. They can precisely and with no hesitation echo or repeat TV commercials, music, rules, and facts exactly as they heard them the first time. This is known as *echolalia*. We know these echoed words are purposeful, because they are generally repeated at very specific times. For example, when Mary was frustrated and upset, she would hit the nearest person. To stop this troublesome behavior, she was loudly told, "Don't hit!" The next time Mary became frustrated and upset, she began to hit as she said very loudly, "Don't hit!" But, she continued to hit. She had associated the command to the feelings of frustration without understanding the conventional meaning of the words.

But, we also know that the words or sounds have not been processed for meaning because the vocal quality, emphasis, and tempo of the original are all a part of the echo. One young man loved to play his tape recorder. He had memorized all of the songs and could sing them exactly like the recording. However, he also could sing fluently along with the rewinding tape—he included the whirs, squeaks, and squawks, as if they were real words.

Another indication that these echoed words are not analyzed and used with typical meaning is the differences in fluency and quality of the speech. The echoed words are fluent, with intonation and emphasis that matches that of the original speaker. Self-generated speech is generally labored, hesitant, and without expression. It also will show little variety; words may be used in unusual ways and sentence structure may be unusual.

- These children have difficulty understanding the concepts and language of time. Words such as *in a minute, in a little while, soon,* and *later* are nonspecific and virtually meaningless to those with autism. Waiting is one of the hardest things for these children. The inability to predict when things will begin and end can cause extreme anxiety. Many of these children who can speak will ask repeatedly, "When will it be time to . . . ?"

- They are unable to understand the social, language, and cultural aspects of their community without being taught. Those with autism are simply not "hot-wired" to learn these very basic lessons automatically, as do normally developing babies and toddlers. This is perhaps the most basic difference between those with and without autism; some of the first, more important symptoms of autism are in these areas. For example:

  - Those with autism do not automatically learn that other people have value as sources of information, assistance, comfort, or fun. In fact, most of these children do not automatically learn about communication (a) that one person can send a message to another person for some purpose, or that they themselves can initiate an interaction, and (b) that you can send and receive messages with your eyes, facial expressions, gestures, and words.

  - These children are baffled by the perspective and actions of others. They seem not to know what others know and think, or even that people may know and think different things. They seem not to have any idea how or why other people know what they know, nor do they automatically understand why others do the things they do. Although they can learn many of these skills and rules, they rarely learn to use them smoothly and flexibly, especially when under stress.

- They do not easily or meaningfully learn the subtle social and cultural rules and rituals that typically developing children learn automatically. We can teach these children to follow specific rules in specific situations, but they rarely learn to apply or modify the rules for different situations. Those with autism act as if they believe that a rule should be applied in exactly the same way every time in exactly the same situation, but no other; or they seem to believe that the same rule should be applied in exactly the same way to every similar situation.

  One young girl wandered about the room, picking up and dropping objects. With a loud and sharp, "No!" paired with physically holding her hands down, she was taught, "Hands down." She learned this so well that she stopped using her hands. This is a situation when a strategy that may work for most children will backfire when used without understanding how those with autism process information. She had to be taught to use her hands in many different situations. One adult with autism indicated that if someone told her something, it was true in every situation unless that same person told her differently.

- Those with autism do not automatically learn that words have meaning or that words are for communication:
  - That a single word can have more than one meaning (e.g., the color blue, I feel blue, the wind blew, the balloon blew up, and so on).
  - That a single person or thing can have more than one label (e.g., bucket, pail; or Elizabeth, Liz, Mother, Mrs. Brown, my wife).
  - That emphasis, intonation, and sarcasm changes the meanings of words.

  Just think about the difficulty these children must have with pronouns (you, me), prepositions (up, beside, over, on), and words that are spelled differently, but sound the same (I/eye, there/their, to/too/two).

- ♦ They understand and use language in very concrete, literal, and inflexible ways. This is a very important concept. When we try to identify the reason for a child's behavior, we must interpret the situation in the most concrete and literal way possible. As a general rule, those with autism will do exactly what they are told, exactly as they understand it. For example, when one child was told to keep his eye on the ball, he placed the ball against his eye. When the class was told to keep their eyes on the teacher, the child with autism went to the teacher and placed his eyes against her stomach.

- ♦ Children with autism have difficulty understanding and manipulating abstract information that depends on the context or situation for its meaning. The inability to analyze information makes it difficult to reason, compare or contrast ideas, make judgments, adapt a rule to match the demands of different situations, or generate and evaluate alternatives in order to solve problems. Temple Grandin has said that she was unable to hold two things together in her mind at the same time unless she could visually see them together on paper.

When you and I have a problem, we can generate many different solutions. We can evaluate these solutions and select the most reasonable option. In contrast, those with autism have very limited solutions to solve the many different problems they encounter each day (see Figure 3).

FINAL THOUGHTS

Those with autism often are confused, anxious, and frustrated. To better understand their situation, let's assume that their brain works much like a supercamera with the capability to take both pictures and videos. This camera has special sensors that enable it to record the visual and audi-

Most people can generate multiple solutions to a single problem, as illustrated in (3a); but those with autism, who have difficulty generating solutions, must depend on limited or single solutions to solve the many problems faced each day; see (3b).

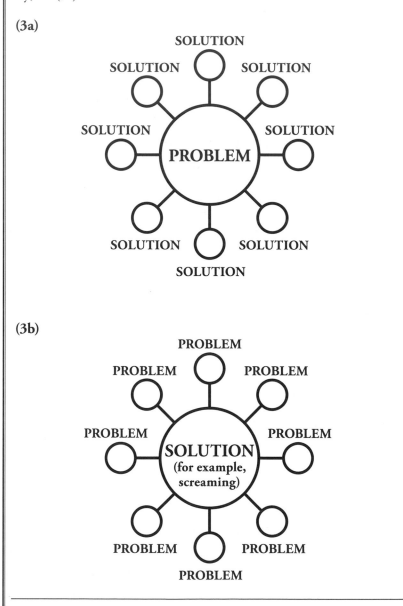

(3a)

(3b)

FIGURE 3. Example of difference in ability to solve problems.

tory aspects of an event as well as the co-occurring odors, tastes, and feel of stimuli present in the surrounding area, in the room, down the hall, or outside the window. But, this camera is not perfect. It does not have the capacity to hone in on or highlight the most salient or meaningful elements in the scene or modulate the input; nor can it automatically edit or label the picture or video before filing.

If you were a gestalt processor, what would your camera record at this moment? It would record all of the co-occurring stimuli—not only the sights, sounds, odors, flavors, and tactile experiences surrounding you, but the intensity of that stimulation in the situation you are in right now. Say that you are talking on the telephone. Simultaneously, your camera would record the bright light from the window making lines on the floor and glistening from dust particles in the air, the feeling of the scratchy label on the neck of your shirt, the sound of the truck on the street, the odor of paint from the garage, the neighbors talking outside your window, and the sounds and moving lights from the TV. You can see how confusing the world is likely to be for your child with autism.

Have you used a video camera? Think about the irrelevant and confusing material recorded on your first videotapes. Before I was totally in control of the On and Off switches, my first tapes include snatches of events—snapshots of a moment caught in the middle of an event. Some long sequences were recorded that began in the middle of one event and continued through to the middle of the next event. I have many stretches of tape showing the carpet or the sidewalk as I walked about thinking the camera was turned off. Interestingly, those snatches of carpet and sidewalk also include the conversations and noises going on nearby that do not relate to the recorded picture.

Do you have a box of unlabeled and unedited pictures and videotapes in your closet? If so, you know how hard it is and how long it takes to find a specific picture or specific sequence on a videotape. It is no wonder that children with autism have a hard time retrieving sequences of information in the correct order.

If your sensory system worked differently and inconsistently, you might be able to do something at one time but not another. If you could see, hear, smell, and feel the stimulation from the environment, but could not make sense of it, what would you need in order to learn and manage yourself in this culture, this environment?

Autism is a sensory disorder; so for a moment, let's think about the needs of those with other sensory disorders—those who are deaf or blind. Those who are deaf can see but not hear. They need an interpreter to give them information, to call attention to events outside their vision. Those who are blind can hear but not see. They need not only an interpreter, but also a guide. My dictionary defines an interpreter/guide as one who restates in clear language to convey meaning; one who assigns meaning to events, actions, or intentions, and shows the way. An interpreter/guide highlights critical information and directs the effort.

Because those with autism often cannot make sense of the environment, they also need interpreters and guides to organize the environment and provide information in forms that they can understand. This is our role. These highly concrete and visual individuals need us to provide information about their world in a concrete and visual format. (For strategies for interpreters, see Chapters 9 and 10.)

Finally, after all of the discussion of deficits and problems, it is important to remember that your child with autism is a valuable person with needs and feelings just like other children. The situation may not be what you had previously envisioned, but with appropriate early intervention, ongoing education, and support, your child will be able to make contributions to society and live a satisfying life.

PARENTS AS ADVOCATES 3

Ａt this time, when you are trying to adjust emotionally to the reality that your child has autism, you may be inundated with conflicting feelings, information, and advice. It may be easier to deal with these contradictions if you understand how they came about.

UNDERSTANDING CONTRADICTORY INFORMATION

There is little in the world that is certain. Contradictory and competing ideas are the rule in education, child rearing, medicine, politics, religion, economics, and almost every other field.

Autism is very complex disorder with a relatively short history. There still is much we do not know about the condition. Theories are developed in an attempt to clarify the issues, and people become emotionally involved in the support or rejection of one theory or another. It takes a long time to conduct research, publish it, and have it verified or discredited. It takes even longer to put research into practice. Many years must pass before we know the long-term effects of a treatment.

Two other issues contribute to the mass of conflicting information. First, it is sad to say, sometimes research is manipulated to support or reject a specific theory—especially when there is money to be made. Although most researchers are conscientious and use valid research methods, the potential for manipulation is true in all fields. Children used in research projects may be selected in such a way as to get a specific result, and those children may be very different from your child. In other situations, the research design is questionable, so that the reported findings may not be valid. Some studies are conducted by researchers who are pressured to achieve quick results, so the issue being studied may be so refined that it has little if any relevance to the larger field; or the period of the study is so short that long-term results are unclear.

Finally, there is no system for discarding—or even labeling—material that has been discredited or refuted. Books are written and the media report bits and pieces of research, opinions, and miracles. Libraries purchase and keep this material, so that it appears to have equal weight with the new and validated information.

Although these factors may explain the contradictions, you continue to have many questions, and it doesn't really help to discover that there are not many easy answers. You still are faced with making decisions about interventions at the same time that you simply are attempting to keep your family going and manage the day-to-day care of your child. If your child had an ear infection, antibiotics would be prescribed; if your child were deaf or hearing impaired, hearing aids and sign language would be recommended treatments. But, with autism, there is no one universally accepted treatment.

Instead, you are confronted with the need to be an advocate, to study, to make decisions about the treatments your child may need, and to monitor those treatments. This is a very demanding role, one for which in all likelihood you have not been trained.

GUIDELINES FOR THE PARENT ADVOCATE

The following eight guidelines will help you during this transition from a parent with a child who has some problems, to the role of a parent who has a child with the problems of autism. As you will soon see, you will be working on all of these tasks at the same time you are carrying on your other family duties.

Guideline 1: Educate Yourself About Autism

Your first job is to find and evaluate information about autism. There is probably more conflicting information about autism and the treatments for autism than for any other disability. Local libraries and bookstores may or may not have current information. Books and articles about autism are of seven general types listed below. Among the many helpful books and journals available, a few specific references are suggested that will likely match your needs at the beginning stages of your search.

1. Reports of individual research studies (e.g., *Journal of Autism and Developmental Disorders*).

2. Edited books with each chapter written by a different author reporting different strategies or studies (e.g., *Preschool Issues in Autism*, by Eric Schopler, Mary E. Van Bourgondien, and Marie M. Briscol [1993]).

3. Family stories that describe a single individual with autism, parents' efforts to obtain appropriate services, and the child's responses to various treatments (e.g., *Without Reason: A Family Copes With Two Generations of Autism*, by Charlie Hart [1989]).

4. Personal experiences with autism written by adults with autism (e.g., *Thinking in Pictures: My Life With Autism*, by Temple Grandin [2006]).

5. Basic overviews with advice and resources for parents (e.g., *Facing Autism: Giving Parents Reasons for Hope and Guidance for Help*, by Lynn M. Hamilton [2000]).

6. Descriptions of a single program model or intervention philosophy (e.g., *The Child With Special Needs: Encouraging Intellectual and Emotional Growth*, by S. I. Greenspan and S. Wieder, with R. Simons [1998]).

7. Guides that integrate the knowledge about autism with step-by-step processes for identifying and meeting the varied needs of those with autism (e.g., *Understanding the Nature of Autism: A Practical Guide*, by Janice E. Janzen [1998]).

Some of the books may be in your local library or in special lending libraries maintained by state and local special education or parent advocacy organizations. Local bookstores may have some of these titles on their shelves, or they will order them for you. However, there are many different books available that may be of help as you learn more about this topic. Ask your local bookstore to direct you to its special needs section so you can browse various titles.

Evaluating Printed Material. Consider the following facts when evaluating books and articles about autism.

1. Any writing that proposes the theory that autism is an emotional problem caused by parental rejection is outdated and unsound. This theory was proposed before the neurobiological basis of autism was discovered.
2. Although family stories provide valuable and varied perspectives, it is important to consider them in relation to the characteristics of your child with autism, your family values, and your family resources.
3. Material that emphasizes the use of aversives or punishment to eliminate behaviors is outdated and of questionable value for children with autism. See Chapter 9 for behavior management strategies that match current best practices.

Guideline 2: Seek Help From a Professional Advisor or Advocate

Find a professional advisor with whom you feel comfortable, and who can support you and provide you with additional autism resources. This professional could be employed at the evaluation center where you child was diagnosed, or it might be a staff member of the local early intervention or special education program in your local school district, parent advocacy center, or office for developmental disability services.

A professional advisor can guide you through the systems to get the services your child will need. There generally is a different process for obtaining services in each state or local community. Check to be sure that this person has recent experience with young children with autism. Ask questions, and do not be afraid to stop a meeting or a discussion to ask the professional to explain or clarify the terms he or she uses. You have a right to understand all you can about your child and his needs if you are to effectively monitor his program and advocate for appropriate services.

Guideline 3: Locate a Parent Support Group

You will need to meet with other parents of children with autism. If an autism group is not nearby, groups for parents of children with other developmental disabilities can be helpful. However, unless other parents have had direct experience with autism, they rarely truly understand many of the issues you will face. You will need a group in which you feel comfortable expressing your honest feelings and fears, knowing that they will be understood.

Parent groups are not only a source of emotional support, but also a source of valuable information. Experienced parents will know how to maneuver through the different systems and agencies in your community to get the services your child will need. These parents will know which doctors and dentists understand and work well with children with autism, and they can share their experiences with different treatments.

One caution, however: Remember that each child with autism is unique and each family is different. Parents are a good source of information, but a treatment that made a significant difference for one child may not match the needs of your child. The experiences of others are important for your consideration, but again, your personal decisions must be based on your child's specific characteristics, your family's values, and your emotional, financial, and physical resources.

You can find out about local parent groups by visiting the Autism Society of American (ASA) Web site (http://www.autism-society.org). ASA has chapters in every state and publishes *The Advocate*, a quarterly magazine. The organization also sponsors a major conference every summer, in addition to regional conferences at various times and locations. You probably will want to join this excellent organization.

Guideline 4: Take Care of Yourself and Your Family

Although your child certainly has many needs, he especially needs his family to be emotionally and physically healthy. If you have other children, they will be concerned, fearful, and even a bit lost because so much of your energy is—and needs to be—focused on your child with autism. Part of your energy also is being taken by the grieving process that all parents endure when first discovering that their child has a disability.

This is a particularly stressful time for everyone in your family. They, too, are grieving and making adjustments. It could be the prime time to locate and participate in family counseling or other family support networks. But above all, talk to your mate. When couples mutually share and accept feelings and concerns, when they support each other and work together, each person is strengthened.

Involve your extended family. Grandparents, aunts and uncles, and friends and neighbors need information about autism. They need to know how to help, for you will need help. This is particularly important for single parents.

Try to find time for yourself. If you are to maintain the energy you will need over the long term, you need time to recharge your batteries. Periodically arrange with family, friends, or a respite care provider or service to take care of your child and give you some time to be alone, to exercise, to engage in a hobby, or have time with your spouse, friends, and your other children.

Parents who understand how vulnerable and difficult their child can be often are afraid to trust another person to provide respite care. But, quality trained respite care providers are available who can keep your child safe, and safety is the critical issue in the short term. If you live in an area without a respite care network, enlist a willing relative or friend. Have that person spend time in your home to see how you manage and how you continually check your child's safety. Then spend some time in that person's home so your child feels comfortable when you leave. Your child may become upset and the respite provider may not do things in the same way that you do, but your child will feel safe and will not suffer long-term damage from periodic changes like these. In fact, as an advocate, you must think in the longer term. If you or a family member should become ill or have a major accident, it will be to your child's advantage to be accustomed to staying with other people.

Above all, take one day at a time. Live with the reality of today, and avoid dwelling on the "what ifs" and the "what thens" of the future. Look for and cherish the good things and the small, humorous events that happen each day.

Guideline 5: Organize Your Child's Life

We know enough about those with autism to know that these children are happier, more relaxed, and more purposeful when there is order in their lives. When they understand what is going to happen, they are easier to live with. Ask your child's teacher or case manager for training and help in setting up structure in your child's life. When you teach your child to live and work independently within that structure, life will be easier for the whole family.

Your child will benefit by being treated as normally as possible and included in family leisure activities. But, your child also needs to learn that other people can care for him as well, that sometimes he does things with friends or relatives without his parents. This is true in all families, whether or not autism is an issue. Ensuring that your child gets plenty of vigorous exercise at least once each day provides opportunities for the child to release tensions and feel more relaxed in the house. Although changing routines and adding new experiences can cause stress, your child can and must learn to tolerate these interruptions in his life. With forethought and planning, these experiences can be fun and productive.

Some strategies for setting up structures and preparing the child for changes are described in Chapters 9 and 10.

Guideline 6: Set Priorities and Ask for Help

There are times when your child's needs must take priority; when you must spend a great deal of time and effort on making sure he has appropriate services and care. Early intervention and special education services generally make provisions for a support team. Once you develop trust and a good working relationship with this team, there will be times when you can let go a little—at least, for a short time—and focus on your other priorities. Remember that all families must set priorities and vary their focus and energy to address their top priorities at any specific time.

Guideline 7: Keep Track—Start a File

Not only are you your child's parent, interpreter, and advocate, you also are the manager of information. If you have not already set up a simple file system, do so as soon as possible. It will save you considerable time down the road. Keep medical records, records of developmental milestones, reports of evaluations, and records related to your child's service plan.

Pieces of this information will be needed whenever your child is referred for a major evaluation and as he grows and needs more or different services. These records also will be needed if it becomes necessary for you to advocate more forcefully for appropriate services for your child. Keep these records into adulthood; they will be invaluable if you have to prove that your child's problems have been present from an early age.

It also is important to record some of your observations—the little things you notice. A periodic review of these notes can provide the clues for you and your child's teachers to predict and prevent or resolve learning and behavior problems, as well as medical problems, and to see progress.

You may want to keep track of your observations in a loose-leaf notebook. Your notebook could include a section for recording anecdotes related to a serious upset or how your child participated in a family activity. Another section could contain lists to track changes in communication, behavior, growth, and new skills. Some parents need to keep records of their child's responses to medications and food sensitivities. Other lists could include the following:

* *Things your child likes, tolerates, and dislikes.* Set up three columns to list things such as foods, toys, activities, people, locations, and special interests. This is critical information for you and your child's teachers.
* *Things that trigger problems.* Include sensitivities to noises, making a mistake, or being told over and over to do something.
* *Things that are calming.* Does your child become calm when being rocked, having a drink of water, or sitting in a beanbag chair?
* *How your child communicates.* List the subtle ways your child lets you know what he needs or how he feels (e.g., "Today, he did this . . . and it means this . . .").

Be sure to keep the information current, and include the date on all entries.

On a day-to-day basis, you and your child's teacher need to know about events that may have an impact on your child's behavior. When a child is unable to share information, it is difficult to find things to talk about. For example, if you know that a police officer visited the child's classroom, you can have a conversation about the visit, perhaps share a book about police officers, or draw a picture of a police officer. If teachers know that Dad will be out of town for several days, or that the child is scheduled to visit the dentist, the event can be discussed at school and some extra support can be provided. One quick way to share this type of information is by means of a small spiral notebook that the child carries to and from school in his backpack. It takes only a moment to jot down a sentence or two. It also is a quick way to send compliments or notes about a new skill that has been mastered.

This type of current daily anecdotal information can help a new teacher or respite care provider learn to understand your child.

Guideline 8: Forgive Yourself

Each family does its best to care for and support all of its members. Stress will sometimes overwhelm you, and occasionally you will make mistakes. Remember that you are only human, and humans are not perfect. In most cases, children with autism will not be permanently damaged by occasional mistakes. Pull yourself together and learn what you can from the mistake. Then move on. You do not have the energy to waste on guilt and regret. Accept your imperfections, try to keep your perspective, and look forward to a new day. As you gain confidence and perspective, you will even begin to see the humor in these situations.

Conclusion

Your role as an advocate will become more comfortable with experience. You also have another role—to continue to love and cherish your child with autism. Value your child's uniqueness and rejoice in each small success, for goals are reached one step at a time. Although it may take some time to realize, you are now engaged in perhaps the most creative journey of your life.

SOURCES OF INFORMATION

Organizations

The following organizations are good sources of information about all aspects of autism.

Autism Research Institute (ARI)
4182 Adams Ave.
San Diego, CA 92116
866-366-3361
http://www.autism.com

ARI is a major source of information concerning new research, programs, and resources related to autism. ARI publishes *Autism Research Review International*, a quarterly newsletter covering the latest research and concerns in the field.

The Autism National Committee
P.O. Box 429
Forest Knolls, CA 94933
http://www.autcom.org

This is a very active advocacy group dedicated to human rights issues.

Autism Society of America (ASA)
7910 Woodmont Ave., Ste. 300
Bethesda, MD 20814
800-328-8476
http://www.autism-society.org

ASA manages an information and referral service, a clearinghouse for information about autism and autism services; publishes *The Advocate*, a quarterly magazine; and schedules an annual autism conference.

Autism Speaks
2 Park Avenue, 11th Floor
New York, NY 10016
(212) 252-8584
http://www.autismspeaks.org

Autism Speaks is dedicating to funding research into the causes, prevention, treatments, and cure for autism; to raising public awareness about autism and its effects on individuals, families, and society; and to bringing hope to all who deal with the hardships of this disorder.

Indiana Institute on Disability and Community
2853 E. 10th St.
Bloomington, IN 47408
(812) 855-6508
http://www.iidc.indiana.edu

This institute offers many resources for teachers, parents, and other service providers.

Autism Journals and Periodicals

Autism: The International Journal of Research and Practice (Sage; http://www.sagepub.co.uk/journalsProdDesc.nav?prodId=Journal200822)

Focus on Autism and Other Developmental Disabilities (Sage; http://foa.sagepub.com)

Journal of Autism and Developmental Disorders (Springer; http://www.springer.com/psychology/child+&+school+psychology/journal/10803)

PART II
TREATMENTS AND SERVICES

TREATMENT DECISIONS 4

Autism research has expanded rapidly in the last few years and is yielding promising—even exciting—information that may ultimately lead to the prevention of autism. More effective and safer drugs for treating many of the symptoms or conditions that commonly occur with autism (such as hyperactivity, seizures, obsessive-compulsive behaviors, and high anxiety) also are being studied.

TREATMENT OPTIONS

At this time, the only treatment that helps *every* child with autism is a structured early intervention and educational program. Over the years, numerous other treatments and therapies were developed that have helped some children with autism. See Figure 4 for a list of treatments that are most commonly referred to in the autism literature.

Each of these treatments has some parent and professional proponents, yet none of the treatments are helpful to every child with autism; in fact, some treatments may have a negative effect for some children. To complicate your decision making, none of these treatments have conclusive supportive data that clarify which children might be helped.

It is important for you to be alert to new discoveries in the field and to keep an open mind as you investigate new treatments and strategies. But, when the data are contradictory, decisions should be made with caution. When you consider using a new treatment or therapy with your

- Structured education and early intervention
- Medications/drugs to treat symptoms
- Anti-Yeast therapy
- Vitamin/Dietary approaches
- Auditory integration training
- Communication/Language therapy
- Sensory integration therapy
- Occupational therapy
- Relaxation training
- Music therapy rhythmic entrainment
- Visual training
- Colored lenses
- Osteopathy/Craniosacral therapy
- Holding therapy
- Patterning (doman/delacato)

FIGURE 4. Treatments most commonly mentioned in the autism literature.

child, you will want to gather enough information so you can make the decision with confidence that it cannot hurt your child, and it might help. So, begin your investigation as a hopeful skeptic (if there is such a thing).

EVALUATING TREATMENTS

Consider the following guidelines for evaluating research, treatments, therapies, program models, or intervention strategies before making decisions that will have a major long-term effect on your child and your family. These are only some of the issues to consider when evaluating the potential value of a treatment for your child. You may think of other questions. This is not intended to collect only yes or no answers, but to guide your thinking as you gather relevant information. The questions are not intended to automatically rule out (or rule in) any particular method of treatment. Rather, the information can help you analyze and balance the costs and potential benefits of these treatments for your child and your family.

Guideline 1: Basic Cautions

When evaluating treatments and interventions:

- if a treatment sounds too good to be true, it probably is;
- if it offers, suggests, or promises a cure, be very cautious; and
- if it requires costly expenditures of money or time, be especially cautious.

Guideline 2: Questions to Guide Decisions

Before making decisions about new medical or educational treatments, consider these questions:

- What are the intended outcomes of successful treatment?
  - Does that outcome match your child's need?
  - Do the potential outcomes address your child's goals?

- What are the possible long-term effects or risks if the treatment does not work? Consider issues such as:
  - the potential physical side effects of drug treatments,
  - the loss of important teaching/learning time, and
  - restrictions of activities or food.

- Are the requirements of the intervention or treatment consistent with your family values and resources?
  - Will the treatment or interventions be painful to your child?
  - Will you feel comfortable using the strategies or the interventions in your own home?
  - Will you feel comfortable watching others use the strategies with your child?
  - Do you realistically have the emotional, financial, and energy resources to follow through with the treatment without putting your family life in jeopardy? How would this treatment fit with other family priorities?

- How will you know whether your child is making progress or improvement?
    - What is your child's current rate of progress under the present conditions? (This can be determined by an assessment or reassessment of your child's level of functioning by current program staff members or at an evaluation center.)
    - Who will monitor progress, and how will it be monitored? Are your child's important goals being monitored?
    - Are there other possible explanations for any noted progress with the new treatment? (For example, could the progress be related to co-occurring instruction, therapy, or experiences, or a change in the home situation?)
    - How soon should it be possible to see progress?
    - How long should the treatment be continued if no progress is noted?
    - How can you monitor your child's gains at home? Can you keep track of the number of tantrums, the number of nights your child sleeps all night, or the number and quality of interactions with family members before and during any treatment change?
    - What are the risks if you decide to discontinue the intervention?

- What other treatments or services would be available if you choose to discontinue the intervention?
- What do other parents and professionals think of this treatment?
    - If you are considering a new drug, check with your child's pediatrician about side effects of the treatment. If it is an alternative treatment, most (but not all) physicians are skeptical. It is especially important to check on the possibility of negative drug interactions or other complicating medical factors. Also ask your pharmacist to review a list of prescription drugs, over-the-counter

drugs, and vitamins and minerals that your child is currently taking or that you are considering.

- What was the response of your child's case manager, teacher, and other therapists? Has he or she worked with other families whose children were involved in the treatment?
- Have you talked with parents whose children responded positively to this intervention or treatment? Have you talked with parents whose children made no progress or lost skills during this intervention? Are the characteristics of their children similar to your child's characteristics?

- Check the literature. Has this treatment been discussed in *The Advocate* or *Autism Research Review International*? Has the intervention been discussed in a peer-reviewed journal?
- How is your child progressing with his current intervention program? It is important to know your child's current level of functioning before you start a new treatment so you can measure changes in skills and/ or behaviors.

Guideline 3: Study the Research Data

Study the data to determine whether the conclusions are relevant to your child. Initially, you may want your professional advocate or pediatrician to review the research with you.

- Determine the ages and descriptions of the children involved in the study.
- How were these children selected? By random selection? By parents who could pay to have their child in the study? By level of intellectual ability? By the presence or absence of specific symptoms or characteristics?
- How were the children tested before and after the study? Were the testing procedures valid for those with autism?

- Does the report describe the characteristics of the children who made progress? The characteristics of those who made less or no progress?
- Does the report describe negative effects and the characteristics of the children who had negative effects?
- Are the results both statistically significant and therapeutically valuable or relevant? The one does not necessarily guarantee the other.
- Is there follow-up data to determine whether the benefits were lasting or generalized after 6 months? One year? Five years?

Once you have the information, it may be helpful to do a cost/benefit analysis. Sort your information and list it under either a column headed "Positive" or a column headed "Negative." In general, children benefit most when select treatments are used in combination with a structured educational program designed to address the unique needs of children with autism. It can be dangerous to focus on only a single method or treatment, especially if critical functional skills, communication skills, and/or social interaction skills are ignored or delayed.

Temple Grandin noted that there are no miracles or cures for autism. She cautioned parents to avoid being misled by the claims of people who promote their own specific therapies or programs. She emphasized that effective treatments require a reasonable amount of effort and can be provided without spending large amounts of money. Grandin also reminded us that any treatment or program that has helped one child "may be useless for another." For more information, see her recent book, *Thinking in Pictures: My Life With Autism* (Grandin, 2006). (These issues will be discussed in more detail in Chapters 6 and 7.)

Finally, consider the thoughts of Elizabeth Gerlach, a mother of two sons, one of whom has autism. She noted:

Living with autism is like running a marathon not a sprint; and it is important that we do what we can, when we can, and not feel guilty if we aren't trying the latest treatment. . . . Yet, as parents of children with autism, we cannot afford to sit back passively and hope our children learn by osmosis or "get better" on their own. People must choose treatments and educational opportunities that best fit the needs of their child and their family. We must choose wisely, and to do that requires research and asking many questions. We must often fight hard, uphill battles with school districts, insurance companies, and other bureaucracies. Because of this, it is critical to have support for our choices from family, friends, and service providers. . . . There is no Magical Mystery Cure, but we must not give up hope for greater understanding of the nature of autism and effective treatments to relieve its symptoms. (Gerlach, 1998, p. 7)

EDUCATIONAL SERVICES 5

Prior to 1975, schools had no mandate to provide services to children with disabilities. These children usually were excluded from public school; or, if they were included, there was little knowledge about how to provide them with the appropriate services to ensure that they would become more independent in their local community. Students with autism were most often kept at home, where their parents, without support, tried to educate or train them. Most often, these children were ultimately institutionalized. Parents who had the financial resources could find private programs for their child. These programs generally required parents either to travel great distances each day, move their families to be closer to the program, or depend on a program that had residential services.

The situation changed when the Education for All Handicapped Children Act of 1975 was passed that mandated appropriate educational services for every child with a disability. In contrast to the time when most children with autism were seen as virtually uneducable and unable to achieve any level of independence or productivity, today they are living much more independently with varying levels of support. As a result of that first law, we have learned a great deal about autism.

INDIVIDUALS WITH DISABILITIES EDUCATION ACT

It is important that you understand the provisions of the current law, the Individuals with Disabilities Education Act (IDEA; 1990). You can obtain copies of the law, which was amended in 1997 (PL 105-17) and 2004, and your state's administrative rules from the special education department of your local school district or from the state education agency or department. This information also can be located on the Web. Carefully note the meaning of all acronyms. If they have not already become a part of your life, they soon will.

General Provisions of IDEA

Federal laws are complicated and much too long for most of us to read easily. In fact, the 1997 amendments to IDEA fill 157 pages. This law has several parts, but we are most concerned about two of them:

- Part B provides for special education for all children with disabilities from age 3 through age 21. Each child's program is defined in an Individualized Education Program (IEP).
- Part C addresses Early Intervention (EI) for infants and toddlers with disabilities from birth to age 3. Each child's program is defined in an Individual Family Service Plan (IFSP).

This law specifies certain procedural safeguards that schools must follow. These safeguards keep parents informed and give them the right to participate in making decisions about most aspects of their child's program. There also is a process for parents to follow if they disagree with aspects of their child's program (see discussion of due process, p. 61, and home/school conflicts, pp. 125–129).

Early Intervention Services

Early intervention services are provided by agreement between public schools and other agencies. Although these arrangements will vary in different states and regions, your pediatrician or child evaluation center probably will be able to give you information about the process for obtaining EI services for your child. You also can obtain information from your local school district office or from regional and state educational agencies.

EI services can be provided at your home, a childcare center, or other setting. Services are designed to be developmentally appropriate for infants and toddlers. These services are developed with you and described in an IFSP. Services can include evaluations, home visits to provide training and support to parents, and the services of specially trained teachers, speech-language pathologists, occupational therapists, teaching assistants, and others who address the individual child or family needs. There is a family service coordinator to ensure that programs are developed and implemented and that the provisions of the law are followed. That person coordinates all services across the various agencies and acts as the central contact in helping parents obtain the services and assistance they need.

Special Education Services

Although the law includes many provisions and procedures for serving children with disabilities ages 3–21, I will summarize five of the basic provisions that will drive your child's programs.

Free and Appropriate Public Education. All children with disabilities ages 3–21 are entitled to a Free and Appropriate Public Education (FAPE). This includes special education and related services at no cost to the parents. Related services include speech-language therapy, physical or occupational therapy, assessment and psychological services, transportation, and other services. This law has been interpreted to define *appropriate* as the type and level of service to ensure that the child makes progress toward meeting goals and objectives. The law does not necessarily promise the most appropriate program (i.e., the most highly advertised or the most expensive). For children with autism, the definition of an appropriate educational program often is debated and has led to a number of hearings and court cases (see Chapter 6 for elements of an appropriate program for young children with autism).

Assessment Services. Your child will be assessed to determine whether he is eligible for special education services and to determine his current level of functioning for program planning. The law stipulates that the assessment must be conducted in the child's primary language and must have no cultural or racial bias. In addition, eligibility for special education depends on more than one assessment procedure (or test), and the determination must be a team decision.

You need to know that there is a difference between a *diagnosis of autism* and a *determination of eligibility for special education services.* A pediatrician or a psychologist can make the diagnosis of autism if a child has the symptoms that meet those outlined in the *DSM–IV–TR* (see pp. 8–10).

Eligibility for special education services depends on meeting the criteria for autism services outlined in your state's administrative rules. In some states, the eligibility criteria match those published in the *DSM–IV–TR*, but in other states, the criteria are somewhat different. One of the reasons for this is that the American Psychiatric Association periodically revises its criteria and the labels for the subcategories of a condition. Confusing? Yes! But, at this time, individual states are given the right and some discretion to determine how a federal law will be implemented in their area.

As a result of these procedural differences, one of the first things that will happen when you seek special educational services for your child will be the assessment to see whether he meets the special education eligibility criteria for autism. This assessment generally is conducted by at least two of the following: a school psychologist, special education teacher, autism specialist, speech-language pathologist, or other professional person as deemed necessary.

The assessment to determine eligibility is likely to include three parts:

1. A review of previous evaluation reports.
2. An interview with parents to identify (a) differences or discrepancies in the development and use of communication, social, and play skills; (b) any evidence of over- or underreactions to sensory stimuli; (c) unusual interests; and (d) inflexible routines.
3. One or more observations of your child in different situations to see how he actually reacts to the environment.

The assessment to determine your child's current level of functioning will include a fairly comprehensive assessment of speech, language, communication, and motor skills; and an assessment of his self-help skills (toileting, eating, dressing, and many other skills).

Least Restrictive Environment. School districts are required to have a continuum of service delivery options available, so that a child with special needs can be educated in the least restrictive environment (LRE). A regular classroom placement may be the LRE for a child if modifications and special services can be delivered effectively in that setting. If the child's needs are such that those services cannot be delivered in the regular classroom setting, a more restrictive setting would be considered the LRE. For example, a 3-year-old child with autism might need an alternate placement if he is so distracted and disturbed by the noises, movements, and confusion of many people in a room that he cannot focus on instruction even with a classroom assistant.

Individualized Education Program. The Individualized Education Program (IEP) is the blueprint for achieving a child's specific goals. This document is an agreement between the school and the parents, and is developed by the IEP team. The law specifies that the members of the team are to include the child's parents, one regular education teacher (if the child is, or may be, participating in regular education), and one special education teacher or provider. The team also must include a school administrator who is responsible for seeing that the IEP is funded and implemented, and an individual who can interpret evaluation results (i.e., a professional experienced in autism). You or the school administrators may invite a parent advocate or others who have knowledge or special expertise regarding the child's needs to participate.

Developing the IEP is a collaborative process. As one of the members of the team, you will review assessment information and be involved in determining goals, objectives, placement, and the support services needed for your child to achieve those goals in the LRE. Initially, your local school classroom for children of the same age may be considered for placement. If adequate and appropriate services cannot be provided in this setting, the team will select a placement in which your child's goals and objectives can be addressed and where the child will have opportunities to interact with typically developing children, as appropriate.

The IEP is to be reviewed and updated annually, or more frequently if a child's needs change or if he is not making the expected progress.

You may find it helpful to have an advocate accompany you to at least the first few IEP meetings or when there may be disagreements about services. An advocate should be someone you trust—one who has good judgment and knows how public and/or private systems operate and who can provide support and a calming influence (these meetings sometimes can be stressful). If you choose to include an advocate, discuss the issues and your concerns before the meeting. Whether or not you have an advocate, make a written list of your questions and concerns prior to the IEP meeting. During the meeting, take notes and feel free to stop the discussion to ask to have terminology and issues clarified. If you believe the plan is appropriate, the school will implement it as soon as possible. If you think an issue needs modification or if something needs to be added or clarified, make another appointment to meet with the team.

Due Process. School districts and the EI service agencies must follow specific procedures to ensure the rights of the child and the parents. These due process procedures are designed to protect the child from improper classification, labeling, placement, and services. Your local school is required to give you a copy of these due process procedures in your primary language at very specific times. School personnel also are required to explain them to ensure that you understand the process.

If you have concerns about your child's services, the first step is to talk to your family's service coordinator (in the case of EI) or the special education program administrator. It helps to deal with concerns when they first arise so steps can be taken as soon as possible to resolve the issues and maintain a good working relationship between the parents and the staff. If the concerns are not resolved at that level, other steps are specified in the law and may include mediation, a written complaint to the state education agency, and/or a request for due process hearing.

OTHER PUBLIC SERVICES

Developmental Disabilities (DD) services are available for most children and adults with developmental disabilities. A diagnosis of autism or autistic disorder will make your child eligible. You may apply for these federally funded services at your state, county, or local Department of Developmental Services. One of the most valuable services is likely to be that of case management. The assigned case manager often serves as a family advocate. This case manager knows how the system works, so that once your child's and your family's needs are identified, you will have direction and support to locate the appropriate services. DD services could include assessment, infant stimulation, behavioral intervention, respite care, vocational support, day treatment programs, residential placements, and other services. Funding is available for these services under certain circumstances. It is wise to apply for these services while your child is young, when the diagnosis is clear. Often, it is more complicated to establish the diagnosis in adulthood.

Social Security Income (SSI) is another resource for families. Depending on the family's income, a child with a qualifying disability is eligible for this monthly income payment. Your DD case manager can help you apply for this service, or you can contact your local Social Security office and request application information.

IMPLICATIONS OF DIAGNOSTIC LABELS

At this stage in your child's life, the primary reason for a diagnosis is for you and the service providers to ensure the services that match your child's very unique needs. You may find that some diagnostic terms will be more helpful than others in securing services now and in the future. Valid research studies are dependent upon the fine diagnostic distinctions found in the *DSM–IV–TR*, but in some situations, those distinctions and labels can delay or prevent access to appropriate services.

For example, the federal law mandates a free and appropriate education for children with disabilities, including those with autism, but it says nothing specifically about those with diagnoses of Asperger's syndrome, other Pervasive Developmental Disorders (PDD), or PDD–Not Otherwise Specified (PDD–NOS). If funding were to be limited further in the future, and if professionals are unaware that PDD is actually a synonym for the spectrum of autism disorders, the law could be implemented very strictly and deny services to those with the other labels. You also may find that a diagnosis of PDD, PDD–NOS, or Asperger's syndrome may not qualify your child for DD services unless you can show that the child has a significant disability (e.g., in combination with mental retardation with an IQ score below 70), or unless your pediatrician will accommodate you by writing down the label *autism*.

Terms such as *high-functioning autism* and *Asperger's syndrome* can be misleading because they provide an illusion that the problems are mild and that little support will be needed. This is a problem in some school systems or agencies with few resources that might give highest service priority to the most severe cases. We know that if these "more able" children are to have opportunities to reach their potential, they have as great of a need for support as their lower functioning peers.

This issue is complicated because higher functioning individuals look and act so normal in some situations that many people assume they think and understand like normally functioning children. But, this is not true. These individuals think and act very differently in any situation that requires the ability to make judgments and decisions, solve problems, and understand and use subtle social and cultural rules. Although we call these individuals "more able" and "higher functioning," their autism often causes significant problems in social, vocational, and other important areas of functioning that will likely require at least minimal support over their life span. Therefore, you may need to be quite assertive to ensure that your higher functioning child gets appropriate services.

IMPORTANCE OF MAINTAINING A HISTORY

Some professionals and parents believe that there is merit in purging or destroying records of any history of autism. Some advocates measure the success of their program by the fact that children make such good progress that they no longer "look autistic," and therefore, all of the evidence should be hidden.

I believe that this policy is not only dangerous, but unfair to the child for several reasons.

- Without a history of the child's autism and the intervention services provided, it will not be possible to determine the long-term effectiveness of interventions.

- Although many young children make great progress and the symptoms of autism are not so clearly apparent, there is as yet no evidence that this neurological condition is "cured" for the long term. We have a great deal of evidence to indicate that many children who function very well at ages 5 and 6 show significant problems at various stages of their life:

  - when expectations and pressures are increased at about third or fourth grade;

  - during adolescence, when hormones and the need for subtle social skills increase; and

  - during adulthood, when life becomes complicated by the loss of parents, supports, jobs, illnesses, and other life stresses.

After several years of intensive instruction, one group of children had been determined no longer eligible for autism services because they showed only minimal symptoms of autism. These children were followed for some time to see how they progressed. The final research report (Church & Coplan, 1995) indicated that four of the five children followed through adolescence continued to have significant academic problems, and that it was relatively common for them to pass academic subjects but "fail" in the cafeteria and gym due to their lack of social skills. Researchers found that the students' improvement actually caused additional problems because school staff members were less tolerant of their rigid behavior related to change. These students were thought to be defiant, disobedient, or emotionally disturbed. Without the protection of the autism label, and an IEP, these students were unable to get appropriate services at items of crisis. The final recommendation made by the research group was to maintain the diagnosis and eligibility for services in such future situations. This would allow an IEP that required monitoring services and allow increasing support when needed before crises occur.

When the history of autism is lost, these individuals are vulnerable to misdiagnosis and inappropriate—even dangerous—treatments. For example, one high-functioning young man continued to have social and behavior problems as an adolescent. He was referred to a psychiatrist without record of his history of autism. His new diagnoses included schizophrenia and bipolar disorder, among others. He did not respond as expected to the medications or the counseling provided; in fact, his behavior problems intensified. As these behaviors became more severe, he was institutionalized, more heavily drugged, and spent a majority of time in restraints. Finally, his mother had to sue the state to get him reevaluated and released from the institution and into appropriate services.

Think how you would feel if you had survived a bout of cancer. Would you want your medical records purged of that event? Or, would you want your doctors to continue to monitor the problem and, if indicated, provide treatment quickly? *So it is with autism, which now is a lifelong condition.* Now that autism has lost its stigma, it makes no sense to purge records. Keep in mind, and remind other professionals, that Pervasive Developmental Disorders is a synonym for autism spectrum disorders, or autism. Keep good records of your child's past evaluations and diagnosis. Keep records of autism services provided in school. Keep records of your child's early behavioral symptoms. When he is an adult, he may need to prove that autism is at the root of his problems and the reason certain services should be provided.

Some years ago, I received a letter for a 43-year-old man who believed he had autism. He lived alone and had a good job that he enjoyed, but for years, he had wondered why he was so different from other people. His parents were no longer living, and he had no other family. The only records he could find indicated that once he had an evaluation and received some special therapy, but there was no diagnosis included. From what he told me about his life, it was fairly obvious that he did indeed have autism. This man really wanted to understand why he was the way he was. Although he was financially secure, he needed emotional and social support. Our correspondence ended after I referred him to a support group, but I often wonder how he is.

PART III
EDUCATIONAL
INTERVENTIONS

EFFECTIVE EARLY INTERVENTION

One of the first things you will hear is that it is critical to get your child into an early intervention program. Parents often are pressured to make decisions quickly. Often they are told directly or indirectly that if their child does not get some specific kind of treatment immediately, it will be too late. Conversely, parents may be told that if they get a specific treatment, and do it hard enough and long enough, their child will be cured. Ultimately, many parents end up feeling guilty that they did not do enough of the right thing soon enough.

Your questions mount. Is early intervention really that critical? If so, why? What does appropriate early intervention look like? Let's begin with some information to help you answer these questions.

IMPORTANCE OF EARLY INTERVENTION

We know that the brain and central nervous system of a newborn child are not fully developed. Normally, neurological pathways develop as infants and young children learn from their explorations of the environment and stimulating play with their parents. Brain development is most active during the first 5 or 6 years of life. By that time, most of the major brain structures are in place and ready for more advanced learning. However, young children with autism do not respond in the typical way to the natural stimulation provided through the environment and by their parents' natural and instinctive efforts to play. They spend a lot of time "timed out," lost in repetitive routines of one kind or another, or engaged in repetitive behaviors and tantrums that are the only way they have found to deal with the confusion. These activities do not stimulate more complex brain development.

Children with autism need various kinds of stimulation presented in ways that will (a) keep their attention focused, (b) highlight critical information, and (c) keep them actively involved. The sooner they begin to attend and make sense of their world, the sooner neurological pathways and structures for later and more complex learning will begin to develop and expand. The sooner these children begin to learn positive skills, the sooner ineffective activities and behaviors will begin to fade. Effective intervention does contribute to an increase in scores on intelligence tests. It also appears that early intervention does increase a child's potential. Yes, early intervention is important and earlier is better, but a quality, ongoing education also is critical.

As Gerlach (1998) said, "This is a marathon, not a sprint"; so take one step at a time and pace yourself. Don't try too many new things at once, or you will become overwhelmed and have less energy and resources for the long haul. The stimulation of trying too many new things at once also can overwhelm your child so that he begins to avoid interactions with you. We all know that when a child is upset and avoiding others, it affects the whole family. We also know that those with autism are lifelong learners; there is no critical time when learning stops. But, we do need to take advantage of those early years when the brain is most pliable and open to greater expansion.

EFFECTIVE EARLY INTERVENTION PROGRAMS

So, what does an appropriate, highly structured educational program look like? Although research is continually testing new teaching theo-

1. To value and intentionally initiate interactions and communications with people.
2. To focus attention on critical elements of the environment and maintain active involvement.
3. To learn the language and to communicate effectively.
4. To tolerate change and accept new experiences—to be more flexible.
5. To do things independently without constant verbal direction.
6. To develop self-monitoring and self-management skills.

FIGURE 5. Six critical goals that address the common deficits of autism.

ries and strategies, there has been a great deal of confusion, controversy, anger, and fear in the field of autism. The controversy is focused on this very issue—the definition of an appropriate program. Interestingly, there still are no conclusive data to show that any one educational philosophy, model, strategy, set of skills, or amount of time in instruction will make a significant difference for every child with autism.

Following a survey of nationally recognized preschool programs for children with autism, Dawson and Osterling (1997) reported that there is "little evidence that the philosophy of a given program is critical for ensuring a positive outcome as long as certain fundamental program features are present" (p. 308).

The following eight elements of effective EI and preschool programs were adapted from that report.

1. The Curriculum Addresses the Deficits of Autism

The curriculum goals for a child with autism are the same as for all other children of the same age plus the critical goals that address the common deficits associated with autism. These critical goals are listed in Figure 5. Skills and strategies to achieve these goals are detailed in Chapter 10.

Typically developing children learn these skills automatically, but for children with autism, the lack of these skills causes major problems throughout life. These goals and pivotal skills must take priority from early childhood through adulthood. Pivotal skills are those that have a critical effect on many areas of function (Koegel & Koegel, 1996). For example, teaching a child to initiate an interaction will positively impact most interactions that occur during the day, with many people and in many different settings.

2. The Environment Is Organized and Highly Supportive

In virtually all programs reviewed, skills are "first taught in highly structured contexts in which the child interacts directly with a trained therapist or teacher" (Dawson & Osterling, 1997, p. 316). Instruction then is shifted systematically to natural environments for generalization of skills.

Elements of a supportive, structured environment include:

- staff trained specifically to teach children with autism;
- low teacher/child ratio—one-to-one (1:1) or one-to-two (1:2) during the earliest stages of intervention;
- distraction-free organization of space and materials;
- use of visual strategies to highlight relevant information;
- use of predictable routines;
- generalization strategies that involve only a few small environmental changes at a time; and
- systematic use of prompts and reinforcement.

Organization and structure compensates for many of the processing problems common in autism. A highly structured, predictable, and meaningful environment maintains productive learning, decreases anxiety, and reduces the number and intensity of program behaviors at home and at schools.

3. The Program Addresses the Child's Need for Predictability and Routine

To assist and calm children before changes and during transitions, all programs use some of the following strategies:

- using visual or concrete cues (schedules, calendars, and similar aids);

- giving ample warnings;
- using rehearsal;
- carrying out a familiar routine during a transition; and
- making frequent, but small, changes in routines.

4. Problem Behaviors Are Addressed From a Functional Perspective

The priority for most effective EI programs is to prevent problem behaviors. Prevention is achieved in a variety of ways: increasing involvement in interesting, highly preferred activities and materials; providing choices; and using structure to clarify the environment.

This proactive and functional approach acknowledges that behavior is communication. Appropriate and effective behaviors communicate that "I understand what to do right now." Problem or ineffective behaviors communicate that "I do not know what to do right now. I am confused, or anxious, or scared, or sick." Adults must look at the situation from the child's perspective to interpret the message of the behavior. To solve more complex problems, a functional analysis of behavior and the environment in which it occurs is used to determine an intervention that truly matches the need. (For information on strategies, see Chapter 9.)

5. Transitions Are Structured and Supported

An effective program supports all transitions—transitions from a home program to a classroom-based program, from classroom to gym, from one EI program to another, or from the EI program to a preschool program. Good transition plans begin with an assessment of the new setting to determine which skills will be needed in that setting and which environmental conditions may need modifications to accommodate individual sensory or safety issues. Other components of a transition plan can include:
- teaching needed skills,
- involving parents,

- transferring critical information to the new staff, and
- preparing the child for the transition.

6. Parent Participation Is Encouraged and Supported

Effective programs recognize that a child's success depends not only on the school program, but also on the informed participation of the parents. Parents are a source of critical information, and they help their child to generalize new skills to other settings. Parents need specific skills to prevent and/or manage problem behaviors in the home and community. Some programs require significant commitments from parents; others allow parents to choose how they want to be involved. Effective programs offer parent training and varying levels of parent support that can be accessed at home or at school. There is sufficient evidence that children with autism make greater gains when parents and teachers work together and use similar strategies.

7. Intervention Is Highly Focused and Intense

The number of training hours varied in the programs studied by Dawson and Osterling (1997), ranging from 14 to 40 hours, with an average of 27 hours. All but one program provided at least 20 hours of intervention. Another study (Rogers, 1996) indicated that children appear to benefit most if intervention is started between 2 and 4 years of age, and when intervention involves 15 or more hours per week of focused treatment with very low adult/child ratios over a period of 1 to 2 years.

Another study conducted at the Murdoch Center in Australia (Birnbrauer & Leach, 1993) reported that 4 of every 9 students (almost half) have shown "singes of approaching normal levels of functioning" after 20 hours per week of intensive behavioral training for 24 months. This program at the Murdoch Center is based on the Intensive Behavioral model developed in 1987 by Lovaas at the University of California in Los Angeles.

Dawson and Osterling (1997) reported that it is not possible to determine exactly how many hours of intervention are necessary for a positive outcome, because each child is unique. These studies provide parents with important information to help them evaluate the messages from some service providers who insist that a positive outcome (or cure) depends on some specific number of intensive intervention hours.

8. Additional Features

Most effective programs also include the following features:

- Services of a speech-language/communication specialist and the use of a range of augmentative communication methods.
- Services of an occupational therapist to address sensory and motor issues.
- A system to track a child's response to programs and provide a base for making decisions to continue or modify programs. This often is referred to as a *data-based management system*.

Perhaps the most critical element of an effective program is a well-trained staff that understands the learning differences in autism, knows how to apply behavioral principles to the design and delivery of instruction, and knows how to integrate visual and cognitive strategies. Well-trained staff members also understand how to keep all students meaningfully and actively involved throughout the day.

FINAL THOUGHTS

I believe that those with autism are valuable human beings with feelings, needs, sensitivities, and fears much like other people. They are the most naïve, gentle, and truly honest people in the world. They have the potential for leading productive and satisfying lives, with varying levels of support. Those with autism are lifelong learners, just like the rest of us.

Individuals with autism deserve respect and respectful treatment. They have a right to treatment that honors:

- *Their unique learning and thinking style.* Treatment strategies are selected that capitalize on learning strengths to compensate for deficits, and assessment results are interpreted from the perspective of those with autism.
- *Their autism sensory problems.* Accommodations are made to avoid overwhelming stress while gradually extending their tolerances.
- *Their age and development levels.* Young children have short attention spans and an instinctive need for movement.
- *Their unique interests and fears.* Treatment capitalizes on interests, and accommodations are made to resolve their fears.

The safest and most appropriate educational program for any child, including a child with autism, should be balanced and not rely on a single strategy, approach, or therapy, for when the data are contradictory, it is dangerous to "put all our eggs in one basket."

The highest priority for young children is to learn the critical self-regulation, imitation, interactive social/communication, and thinking skills in the context of structured, interactive play with loving and skilled adults. From my own experience, I have seen these children begin to blossom when engaged in such interactive play sessions. Eye contact increases, and it is actually fun to see them begin to imitate and take turns—to ponder and test their power in new and creative ways. Compliance develops as children are taught the meaning of rules and directions in natural situations. (See Greenspan's Floortime Model, p. 100.)

Active involvement is the critical element of effective early intervention. The child needs to be focused and actively involved in productive activities for a majority of every day. Initially, this requires an individual teacher or teaching assistant to help the child maintain meaningful involvement in the natural activities of peers and in individual work and play sessions. Active involvement also is important at home. There are many ways for parents to periodically interrupt and engage their child in the natural ongoing activities of the family (see pp. 162–166).

The most successful programs are those that encourage respectful, supportive, and cooperative partnerships between the home and the local school; and in which parents and teachers are trained to use the same strategies in school, home, and community settings.

Dawson and Osterling (1997) concluded their report of effective early interventions in autism with the following statements:

> If we were to implement what we now know how to do and to cease all efforts at the development of new methods, it is very likely that approximately half of all children with autism would be able to function in a general education program by the time they reached elementary school age. If intervention methods were initiated at even earlier age, . . . the outcome for children with autism by five years of age would probably be even more promising. (p. 323)

They also indicate that if this were to happen, we would need to revise our predictions for long-term potential, and that perhaps the most important task for researchers is to become better at communicating the current knowledge to service providers and parents.

INTERVENTIONS AND PROCEDURES 7

Y our research and study to learn about autism and effective interventions often can be complicated by professional jargon. The problem is compounded because terms are not always used accurately or precisely. A brief review of the history may clarify some of the terminology issues and help you to understand how strategies are developed.

THE FOUNDATIONS

Essentially, it all began with the scientific study of how people learn. This study of ideas about how learning occurs produced some basic principles or rules now known as *learning theory*. One of the principles is that all learning occurs in a specific sequence that includes a cue that signals or triggers a response or behavior, which in turns triggers a consequence, either punishing or reinforcing. This basic learning sequence is illustrated in Figure 6. An application of this theory, again illustrated in Figure 6, is an example of how we learn from each other—sometimes known as *social learning theory*; whenever there is an interaction between two or more people, the behavior of one person will affect the behavior of another.

As in every field of study, subgroups form to investigate different aspects of a subject. Four groups approached this study from different perspectives: the neurophysiological approach, the information-processing approach, the cognitive/developmental approach, and the behavioral approach (Wolery, Bailey, & Sugai, 1988).

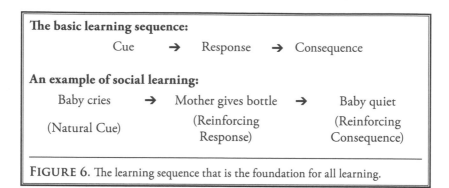

FIGURE 6. The learning sequence that is the foundation for all learning.

Neurophysiological Approach

The *neurophysiological approach* studied learning as it involves the brain structures and the central nervous system. It was determined that as learning occurs, neurological pathways are developed that activate ever more complex brain development and higher levels of learning. We know that most of the major brain and central nervous system structures are in place by 5 or 6 years of age. The results of this approach formed the foundation for early intervention; but there is, as yet, no evidence that any one philosophy of treatment builds neural pathways better or more effectively than any other treatment or model.

Information-Processing Approach

The *information-processing approach* studied the sensory systems (auditory, visual, and so on) and the processes that are involved in learning—what happens between the input of sensory information and the output or resulting behavior. The processes include perception of sensory information, organization and integration of information, storage and retrieval of information, and the transfer of information to produce a verbal or motor response or behavior. Efficient and effective learning depends on the efficiency of the processes and the automatic interactions between the systems. This knowledge is important as we design instruction to accommodate the processing styles of individual children to create strategies that capitalize on processing strengths to compensate for processing deficits. To accurately interpret assessment information and understand the meaning or function of the behavior of those with autism, one must understand their thinking and processing style.

Cognitive/Developmental Approach

Those who established the *cognitive/developmental approach* believed that an individual's behavior is influenced by environmental conditions and by what that person knows or believes to be true about the environment. The word *cognitive* pertains to the mental processes of knowing— perception, memory, reasoning, and judgment. A child's understanding and beliefs about the environment will depend on the stage of cognitive development that has been mastered. For example, if a child has not yet achieved the stage to understand the perspective of others, he will interpret information and behave from his own perspective. This cognitive/ developmental approach requires teachers and parents to plan or arrange the environment so that:

1. The child has opportunities for involvement in activities that are interesting and challenging—activities at the child's level of understanding while stimulating and supporting the next step of development.
2. Growth is promoted through active involvement and interactions with the real environment so children will learn by doing rather than by being told.
3. Feedback is provided as a result of the natural and real consequences of the child's own efforts and actions.

Cognitive teaching strategies are those that provide information in a way to clarify meaning and prevent or correct false beliefs and encourage thinking. When used to intervene in autism, cognitive strategies capitalize on the child's visual strengths to compensate for his inability to analyze and make accurate sense of environmental events, to analyze and solve problems, and to make judgments.

Behavioral Approach

The *behavioral approach* was developed by behavioral psychologists who work under the theory that human and animal behavior can be accurately studied through the analysis of an individual's response to the environment. *Learning* is defined as an observable change in behavior. *Behavior* is defined as any observable activity that can be measured. *Behavioral principles* and *behavioral techniques* were developed from this highly systematic study of the effects of various conditions on learning— the conditions that will build or eliminate specific behaviors. In essence, behavioral strategies involve varying the types of cues, prompts, and consequences and the way in which they are presented to a learner.

Applied behavior analysis (ABA) is a research procedure used by behavioral psychologists to study behavior change; that is, it is used to study the effects of different applications of these behavioral principles to teach important skills and/or to change or eliminate inappropriate behavior. Initially, this process of systematic behavior change was once commonly known as *behavior modification*.

Behavioral techniques provide the foundation for designing and implementing effective instruction. When designing and delivering instruction, teachers must pay attention to:

- the clarity of cues,
- the type of prompts,
- the type of consequences, and
- how to deliver prompts and consequences in the most effective manner.

INTEGRATED APPROACH

It is important to know that the principles derived from all four approaches apply to all people. Every parent and child (or teacher and students) use and are affected by these principles, whether or not they are aware of it. Some of the most effective intervention programs for those with autism integrate the information from all four approaches to learning. The theories and processes described above are automatically in force when typically developing children explore and learn from their environment. However, when a child—for any reason—is unable to learn automatically from the environment, teachers and parents must intervene and take a more active role. They must set up situations (the cues) and provide prompts to ensure that important skills are learned. In autism, the principles must be applied more specifically and carefully if we want positive results.

Note: It is important to know that not every behavioral or cognitive psychologist will have training and experience with autism.

TERMINOLOGY

Below is a list of common terminology that you will want to know.

Behavior Modification

Another term for applied behavior analysis, both are found in the literature to define the process for building new, important skills and weakening or eliminating inappropriate behaviors. The term applied behavior analysis is used more frequently today.

Behavior Management

This term is used in relation to a comprehensive behavior intervention plan. It describes what to do to prevent problems, how to manage problems that do occur, and what to modify or teach so the same problems do not recur. For more information, see Chapter 9.

Cue

A cue is a signal or situation that stimulates or triggers a response. In other words, a cue directs a person to do something. For example, a traffic officer holds up one hand to signal you to stop. Sometimes a cue is called an *antecedent*, a *stimulus*, or an *event*.

Prompt

A prompt is something added or assistance provided to ensure a correct response and prevent an error. The types and the timing of prompts have a significant impact on the child's rate of learning and the generalization of skills.

Response

A response is something added or assistance provided to ensure a correct response and prevent an error. The types and the timing of prompts have a significant impact on the child's rate of learning and the generalization of skills.

Consequence

A consequence is an event that occurs as a direct result of a response—that is, the reaction to the response. The type and timing of a consequence will affect learning, and it will influence the strength of response and determine whether the same response is likely to recur or be modified. There are three basic types of consequences:

- *Reinforcement, reinforcer*—To reinforce is to strengthen or to increase. A *reinforcer* is something *pleasant and valued* given as a result of the response. If a response is reinforced, that response is likely to recur in the same way. The rate of learning new skills, and the strength of those new skills, will depend on the type and timing of reinforcement. It is important to know that inappropriate behaviors also will increase and be strengthened if they are in some way reinforced. For example, a child who is given candy to make him stop crying will likely cry again when he wants candy.

- *Punishment, punisher*—In behavioral terms, a punishment weakens a behavior and decreases the likelihood that it will recur. A *punisher* is something disliked or painful. A punisher can be something as benign as taking away a valued toy, enforcing a brief time-out, or saying "No!" In the past, highly aversive punishers frequently were used in programs for children with autism. Now, aversives are rarely used (but sometimes still remain in a few programs).

- *Correction procedure*—A correction procedure is a response to an error or incorrect response during instruction. A correction procedure directs the learner back to the original cue and provides another chance to make a correct response that will trigger the reinforcing event.

Generalization

Generalization has occurred if a person can learn to use a skill in one situation and then be able to use the same skill when needed in a variety of other situations. If a child learns to ask his teacher for help when he has a problem at school, he must learn to ask other people for help when he has a problem in other settings. Teachers and parents both must work to teach a child to generalize or transfer new skills to other settings and situations.

Intensive Behavioral Intervention (IBI)

This term refers to an intensive treatment model based on the principles of ABA. In this context, *intensive* implies 1:1 instruction for many hours every day (30 to 40 hours per week) over an extended period of time (1–3 years). This model makes use of the *discrete trial* instructional format (see below), and incorporates other behavioral strategies and procedures. Initial skills, such as compliance and imitation, are seen as prerequisites for learning to communicate. An expanded curriculum and more complex responses lead to the ultimate goal of integration with peers. IBI often is used in reference to the early intervention model developed at UCLA by Lovaas (see pp. 99–100). The IBI model has been adopted for use in many autism programs across the country where the procedures may be modified to some extent to match the philosophy and resources of the specific program.

TWO INSTRUCTIONAL FORMATS

As the field of behavioral psychology expanded in the years between 1950 and 1970, research focused on teaching separate and distinct pieces of behavior in very isolated settings. During that period of time, Lovaas reported that the behavioral learning principles (ABA) also applied to children with autism, who previously had been seen as unteachable. This was very exciting news.

As the research continued, a number of instructional formats were developed. In this limited space, we will discuss two of the most commonly used: discrete trial format and incidental teaching format.

Discrete Trial Format

A *discrete trial* is an interactive sequence that includes a cue, a response, and a consequence, followed by a brief pause; it is a distinct and finely defined teaching unit. *Discrete trial training* (DTT), sometimes called *discrete trial teaching*, refers to a systematic repeated practice of consecutive discrete trials to teach a skill to a specific level of mastery. Traditionally, DTT occurs in a 1:1 work session with the therapist facing the child. Initial instruction involves basic skills. Cues are likely to be presented verbally (e.g., "Look at me," "Do this," or "Put in"). Prompts are provided to ensure a correct response, and reinforcement is provided quickly. In this format, trials (opportunities to respond) can be scheduled in several different ways. The two most familiar schedules are:

+ massed trials, in which the same test is repeated in the same way several times in a row (as in Figure 7), and

Teacher (Artificial Cue)		Child (Correct Response)		Teacher (Artificial Reinforcer)
Trial 1				
Claps hands; says, "Do this" (Brief pause)	→	Claps hands	→	Reinforces with arm tickles; says, "Good!"
Trial 2				
Claps hands; says, "Do this" (Brief pause; then repeat)	→	Claps hands	→	Reinforces with arm tickles; says, "Good!"

FIGURE 7. The discrete trial format.

♦ distributed trials, in which related or new tasks are interspersed or presented between the trials.

Note that in teaching situations, the adult arranges the cues, prompts, and consequences to ensure that the child learns the intended lesson.

DTT is only one of the instructional techniques under the ABA umbrella that can be used (applied or modified) to teach many different skills to those with or without autism.

It is important for you to know that when very discrete skills are taught and practiced in isolated settings with a high rate of reinforcement, it takes a considerable amount of time and many trials for the child to generalize those skills and use them functionally in the real world. In fact, if skills are practiced in exactly the same way or in the same situation for too long, it can interfere with generalization. This is especially true with autism. Two studies provided some information about ways to present cues and prompts that particularly pertains to teaching those with autism.

1. One study concluded that it took fewer sessions, trials, and minutes of instruction to master skills when instruction was presented every other day, rather than the every day schedule common in discrete trial training. The differences were especially marked for

the students with autism and PDD, who required 55% fewer sessions to reach criterion, or mastery, with no difference in ability to maintain and generalize skills. This supports an earlier study that indicated that varying tasks (i.e., by either alternating tasks within a session or teaching the task every other day) increased attention and motivation (Venn, Wolery, & Greco, 1996).

2. A study of prompting procedures concluded that it was more effective simply to show a child how to perform a task (passive modeling) and then have the child imitate the task while the instructor used subtle nonverbal prompts (gestures) to prevent errors, than it was to use the more intrusive and traditional hand-over-hand prompting procedure followed by saying something like, "Good job!" (Biederman, Fairhall, Raven, & Davey, 1998).

Incidental Teaching Format

Over time, it was discovered that the concept of the discrete trial format could be modified and applied in many different ways, and that it even could be applied to more natural situations such as in the incidental teaching format. *Incidental teaching* is used by teachers who set up or engineer situations to provide opportunities for the child to practice skills. The incidental teaching procedure also is used to take advantage of teachable moments that occur when the child spontaneously indicates a need or desire. These applications of the incidental teaching format ensure that a child will have multiple opportunities to practice and generalize skills to the real world. Incidental teaching strategies (see Figure 8) are very important for parents to learn and use to help their child generalize or transfer new skills to home and community settings. The engineered approach is set up by the teacher to provide more opportunities for the child to learn and practice a new skill in a variety of situations. Taking advantage of teachable moments is a strategy used when the child initiates an action that indicates a need.

Engineered Approach

Teacher (Engineers cue and waits expectantly)		Child (Responds)		Teacher (Quickly provides reinforcer)
Favorite toy (a bunny) in view, but out of reach	➔	Reaches for toy while saying, "Ooo, ooo, ooo"	➔	Gives toy while saying, "You want the bunny. Here is the bunny."

Taking Advantage of Teachable Moments

Child (Initiates natural cue to signal need)		Adult (Responds)		Child (Is naturally and powerfully reinforced)
Stands at door, crying	➔	"You want the door open to go outside. Say, 'Help.'" Prompt to communicate help, and quickly open door	➔	Goes outside

FIGURE 8. Applications of the incidental teaching formats used in natural context.

OTHER EFFECTIVE PROCEDURES

Because those with autism must be taught so many skills that other children learn automatically, it makes sense to search for more efficient ways to teach. Although the basic principles of learning and behavior remain constant, they are being applied in new ways to teach an increasing number of skills more effectively. In general, new strategies simply involve different ways to set up the basic learning sequence—new ways to present cues, prompts, and consequences to help these children to become more independent. The following strategies are being used effectively to teach children with autism. Notice that these strategies are designed to be adapted to the individual needs of each child.

Pivotal Response Training (PRT)

Pivotal response training (PRT) is based on the ABA principles and involves teaching highly specific skills or responses that are critical to successfully participate in many different situations or tasks. Examples of pivotal responses include learning to respond, learning to persist, learning to self-monitor, and learning functional communication skills (e.g., to initiate requests, to indicate a need for help, or to make choices). PRT depends on the incidental teaching format to teach and generalize critical skills in the context of natural situations. Natural reinforcement is available as a direct result of the child's correct response. This is the most powerful type of reinforcement. For example, a child who persists in requesting help to get a door open is rewarded by being able to go outside. Persistence is an important skill that will enable the child to participate effectively in a broad range of situations and settings with many different people. This is an efficient teaching approach because many small skills are chained together and taught at the same time, and generalization of the critical or pivotal skills is a natural part of the procedure (Koegel & Koegel, 1996).

Structured Teaching

Structured teaching is a systematic process for organizing and structuring the environment, the events, the space, and the time to clarify information for those who see the world from a different perspective. This process capitalizes on the visual abilities of those with autism to compensate for their difficulty in identifying and making sense of the important elements of their environment. The visual structures can:

- clarify and highlight natural cues,
- serves as cues when natural cues are not obvious or are unavailable,
- serve as visual prompts to increase independence, and
- serve as tools for self-monitoring and self-reinforcement.

These structures provide information so the child always knows exactly what to do, when to do it, where to do it, and how to do it. The structures reduce anxiety from distractions and uncertainty, while highlighting critical information to allow the child to complete work and to move from one place to another independently. The process provides a familiar, predictable, and comfortable structure for adding new experiences, thus increasing flexibility and tolerance for change. Learning to use various visual systems independently is indeed a pivotal skill that can be applied to many different activities and settings.

Teaching Functional Routines

This cognitive/behavioral strategy provides a process for teaching many skills in the context of natural daily routines (e.g., eating a meal, going to school, attending a party, or preparing for bedtime). It capitalizes on the natural tendency of those with autism to learn routines quickly and be motivated to repeat familiar routines. Discrete trial, incidental teaching, and structured teaching strategies are incorporated into the design of the instruction and in the process of teaching the total routine. Instruction is designed to teach a total routine that involves knowing:

- when to do it;
- how to begin;
- how to perform the steps of the core skills;
- how to communicate, solve problems, or make necessary choices in the context of the routine;
- how to terminate the routine; and
- how to transition to the next routine.

In order to perform functional routines independently, a child must be able to perform each of these steps independently without verbal or physical prompts.

Interactive Play Strategies

One of the most effective and efficient approaches for addressing the profound social and communication deficits common to those with autism involves interactive lay strategies. If these children are to learn the earliest social interaction skills and use them spontaneously in the natural environment, we must teach those skills in natural contexts from the very beginning.

These strategies are based on the concept that when parents and teachers are more responsive to the child's interests and actions and less directive and dominating, the child with autism will be more relaxed and will increase the time he will interact. In this process, the child also will:

- establish emotional bonds and trusting relationships;
- increase eye contact;
- increase creative play and flexibility;
- expand the number and complexity of interactions; and
- expand his ability to think, reason, and solve problems.

Parents and teachers are trained to conduct 1:1 interactive play or floor-time sessions (Greenspan & Wieder, 1998) several times a day and to use the strategies in all of their interactions with the child at home and at school. The amount of time that the child is intensely and positively involved each day increases dramatically. In fact, these sessions are fun for the adults and the child.

Interactive play strategies and play sessions are but one part of a total balanced program. A number of researchers support the use of these strategies with children with autism (Boutot, 2009a; Greenspan & Wieder, 1998; Klinger & Dawson, 1992).

For information about training, see Greenspan's Floortime Model (p. 100) and see the basic directions for using interactive play strategies (pp. 163–164).

Picture Exchange Communication System (PECS)

This system was designed to develop communication skills in a context of appropriate play and social activities with the child as the initiator. PECS (Frost & Bondy, 2002) is based on the ABA discrete trial and incidental teaching formats, and involves other behavioral strategies as well. Initial training begins at the earliest possible age by noting what a child wants in his immediate environment. The environment is structured to include those basic high-priority items. Initial training involves two staff members, one serving as a communication partner, and the other working behind the child to provide the prompts. As the child reaches for an item (e.g., a cookie), he is prompted from behind (physically guided) to place a picture of a cookie in the teacher's open hand. While receiving the picture, the teacher says, "You want a cookie. Here it is!" The child is given a powerful natural reinforcement as a result of his own actions. Thus, the child learns that communication is powerful, and that he can initiate communication to express his needs. Perhaps even more importantly, he learns that he first must locate and gain another person's attention before he can send a clear message. Many young children with autism master the first critical step of this process during their first day at school. There are no prerequisite skills to begin the PECS program; it begins without first training the child to give eye contact, to imitate verbal or motor actions, or to label pictures. The training expands to teach increasingly more complex communication and social skills. Of all children started on PECS, 82% acquired speech after an average of 11 months of training and continued to use it independently or with augmentation (Bondy & Frost, 1998).

Cognitive Picture Rehearsal (CPR)

This cognitive/behavioral procedure was initially designed to teach and generalize relaxation, visual imagery, self-control, and self-management skills. The process begins with a functional assessment of a problem situation. The next step is to prepare a script that describes:

1. the environmental cues present in the problem situation,

2. the appropriate response, and

3. a pleasant scene to serve as internal self-reinforcement.

Initially, the script is introduced as the child is shown a generic black-and-white line drawing that features him in each scene. Rehearsal also involves visual imagery. For more complete information about this very successful procedure, see Groden and LeVasseur (1995).

Social Stories

This cognitive strategy is used to teach social skills, increase independence, and prevent or reduce problem behaviors. Following an assessment to determine the reason for a difficulty, a short story is developed to describe important social and environmental cues, the perspective of other people in the situation, and a solution or appropriate response to that situation. Once the story is written or pictured in a book format, it is reviewed with the child. The child then rehearses the storybook (or tape) several times independently, or with assistance as needed, before moving on to practice the new responses in the natural situation. This strategy can be applied in many different ways to many different situations; but to be successful, the story must contain certain specific elements. For more information, see Crozier (2009).

THERAPEUTIC APPROACHES

Speech-Language Therapy

The first and highest priority for the young child with autism is to learn to initiate interactions and communicate in some way. Learning the language and learning to speak also are very high priorities, but knowing the words and being able to speak do not ensure communication. Every child needs to receive the services of a speech-language pathologist. The child benefits most when new skills are introduced in 1:1 or small-group situations. Then the therapist shows the teacher and the parents how to use incidental teaching strategies so the child can practice the new skills in many different situations all day long. The focus should be on using language and communication in a variety of settings in which the child may find himself (Wetherby & Prizant, 1999). Services of an augmentative communications specialist also are a high priority—even for those children who can speak—because when these children are in stress, speech does not come automatically, and they may be left with no way to communicate a need for assistance.

Sensory Integration Therapy (SIT)

Autism sometimes is seen as a sensory integration disorder—an inability to process and respond to incoming sensory information efficiently or effectively. This can cause many problems such as oversensitivity, under- or overreactions, and behavior problems. Therapy involves movement activities and various forms of pressure and desensitization activities. SIT is provided by trained and certified occupational therapists (OTs). An occupational therapist with training in early neural development also is able to provide therapy to address the child's sensory problems. Therapy may be provided in a 1:1 situation, and the therapist will help teachers and parents modify natural home and classroom activities to provide the necessary movement and sensory experiences. Therapy to normalize the sensory system helps many children with autism live more comfortably as they learn to tolerate and process sensory information more reliably.

Facilitated Communication (FC)

Facilitated communication is a strategy for providing emotional and physical support to help an individual express needs and ideas by spelling on an alphabet board or by writing or typing on a typewriter or computer. FC is not a communication system, but a way of supporting written communication. This physical facilitation strategy has been used for many years by physical therapists (PTs) to support effective motor movements of those with a variety of neural/motor problems.

Although research has not validated this controversial procedure, some parents report that FC has made a significant difference for their child and their family. One family reported that after their totally nonverbal teenager learned to express himself on a small computer, his behavior problems decreased significantly and he was socially accepted for the first time by peers and extended family members. FC was the strategy used to support David Eastham as he learned to write poetry (see p. 190). Some adults with autism have begun to speak after learning to communicate with FC.

Facilitated communication should be considered if other communication options have not been successful. It is important to note, however, that the procedure can be misused by facilitators who are not well trained.

Auditory Integration Training (AIT)

Although many children with autism have benefited from AIT, it still is unclear how any specific child will respond. Reported benefits include increases in eye contact, spontaneous speech, socialization, and attention span and reduced sensitivity to certain sounds. The design of each child's training program is based on the results of an audiogram. The training involves listening to individually prepared music with earphones for a total of 10 hours (twice a day for 10 days).

Computer Tutorial Programs

Two computer tutorials, *Earobics* (http://www.earobics.com) and *Fast ForWord* (http://www.scilearn.com), may be helpful to some children with autism. The programs were initially designed to improve auditory processing and phonological skills of children with a variety of developmental delays (speech-language disorders, learning disabilities, reading problems, and others). Because many children with autism have these same problems, some parents are interested in these programs. These programs have been used with so few children with autism that it is impossible to determine which or how many will find them useful. In this age of technology, there undoubtedly will be other tutorials and games developed to intervene in various ways.

Before spending money on these computer programs, talk with parents whose children have used them and find out how their children responded. As with other treatments, it is important to know whether the children who had positive responses have characteristics that match those of your child.

A word about using computers: Most children with autism like the visual stimulation of computers. Many children can spend hours at the computer, but when left alone with the computer, they may not spend their time productively. All too often, it is repetitive play similar to the repetitive play that takes their time when off the computer. Some children are just as reinforced or stimulated by error messages as they are by messages that follow a correct response. Once they are left alone to play around with the computer, it is difficult to get them to follow the rules to play or work productively with it. Some professionals have suggested that computers be saved or reserved for only productive work. This means that children must be taught specifically to use a program and monitored to be sure they use it correctly. Computers have the potential for providing useful social and vocational options, but only if the child learns that computers are to be used in specific ways to accomplish something productive.

Other Therapies

There are a number of other therapy-based approaches that have helped some children with autism. They include music therapy, the Doman/Delacato Method, osteopathy/craniosacral therapy, holding therapy, the Squeeze Machine, and many others. For more information about any of these approaches, you can conduct an online search using any Internet search engine.

STAFF AND PARENT TRAINING

A well-trained staff is perhaps the most critical element of effective EI and ongoing educational programs. Training staff members to teach children with autism requires more than a 1- or 2-day autism workshop. If staff members have not had fairly extensive prior training and experience in autism, they generally need a minimum of 5 days of training plus periodic follow-up with on-site consultation and training. Competent well-trained special education teachers often are quick to adapt their skills once they understand the issues related to autism. However, the follow-up consultation is an important element to help teachers apply the new strategies and expand their skills to solve the unique learning and behavior problems of those with autism.

The most efficient and cost-effective training occurs on site. When parents, therapists, teaching assistants, and teachers are trained together, they will speak the same language and they can provide feedback and support to increase the competence of all. In fact, all school staff members—the principal, secretary, cafeteria workers, recess monitors, bus drivers, PE teachers, counselors, and anyone who at some time will have contact with or responsibility for a child with autism—need training for at least half a day. If they understand the basic problems of autism and learn a few basic strategies to help them communicate with the child, their interactions will have a more positive outcome for all.

Autism training may be offered by local, state, or regional agencies, or obtained from nationally recognized training centers. The importance of personnel development (i.e., staff training) is noted in the reauthorization of IDEA, the federal Individuals with Disabilities Education Improvement Act. It is important for parents to check on the school's staff training policy to ensure that their child has well-trained, competent staff members.

MODEL PROGRAMS AS RESOURCES

Effective EI and preschool programs for those with autism vary considerably. The models listed here represent the range of philosophies (e.g., integrated/segregated, intensive behavioral models, relationship-based models) and a range of settings (e.g., statewide public school services, private center-based programs, and university-based centers). Despite the differences, outcomes reported by each of these models were similar, noting that a significant percentage of students had made important gains; for example, significant increases in IQ scores, development of verbal communication skills, reductions in behaviors typical of autism, and others. Note that I did not mention inclusion in general education classes as a significant outcome, because inclusion depends too much on the philosophy of individual public and private programs. Some of the models mentioned below participated in the study of Dawson and Osterling (1997), discussed in Chapter 6. I have had many positive personal experiences with others. All have in some way incorporated the elements for effective programs listed in Chapter 6, and each of these programs has contributed significantly to our knowledge for improving intervention for children with autism.

These programs can serve as resources to you and your local program. Many will provide training to programs in the United States and other countries, and most are willing to send information about their programs. If you are in the area of one of these programs, make an appointment to visit. It can be helpful to see how children with autism respond to different philosophies and approaches.

The Lovaas Institute

This institute was formerly the Clinic for the Behavioral Treatment of Children, a university-based program at the University of California at Los Angeles (UCLA). From this program, Lovaas (1987), published the first evidence that nearly half of the young children who received intense early behavioral intervention (IBI or IEBI) based on the ABA model had made significant gains. Recent research has replicated the same results (Cohen, Amerine-Dickens, & Smith, 2006; Sallows & Graupner, 2005). The treatment model developed at this clinic sometimes is called the Lovaas IBI Model or the UCLA Model. This model actually is a package that includes a curriculum, the intensive treatment format, parent and staff training, and monitoring. For more information about this model, visit http://www.lovaas.com.

Greenspan's Floortime Model

This is an intervention model, not a program site. The Floortime Model is an application of the interactive play strategies for teaching the earliest skills (as described on pp. 92 and 163–164). It is based on the thesis that emotional interactions can stimulate cognitive and emotional growth. The adults' role in the cognitive/behavioral model is to follow the child's lead and play at whatever captures the child's interest while building on his actions in increasingly complex ways that literally compel the child to want to continue the interaction. The process is spontaneous and fun for the child and for the adults. This model is described in detail in *The Child With Special Needs: Encouraging Intellectual and Emotional Growth* (Greenspan & Wieder, 1998).

The model is being introduced into many public and private intervention programs and is being used by an increasing number of families in their homes. For more information, visit http://www.stanleygreenspan.com.

The Groden Center

This private, nonprofit center pioneered the study of relaxation, visual imagery, and cognitive picture rehearsal to teach self-control strategies to those with autism. The center provides an on-site day school, as well as support to individuals who are integrated into local school, community living, and supported employment programs. The program is primarily based on the ABA model, but incorporates many cognitive/behavioral strategies. For more information, visit http://www.grodencenter.org.

Judevine Center for Autism

The Judevine Center in St. Louis, MO, is a private, nonprofit program based on the ABA model. This is one of the first competency-based training programs in the United States. Although the primary mission is to train parents and professionals, Judevine also provides major outreach services for early intervention/preschool programs, public and private schools, and community living and vocational settings in several states and countries. Staff members conduct research on new information and strategies and integrate the best into the Judevine total cognitive/behavioral model. For more information, visit http://www.judevine.org.

LEAP Preschool

LEAP (an acronym for Learning Experiences, an Alternative Program for Preschoolers and their Parents) is one of the first programs in the country committed to serving young children with autism in integrated preschool classrooms with typical children. Staff members in many programs across the United States have received training and are incorporating the LEAP model to serve their children in inclusive settings. For more information, see Strain and Cordisco (1994).

Princeton Child Development Institute

This is a nonprofit agency that offers special education for children with autism, with an emphasis on research as well as service. The program provides a good example of an intensive ABA approach that incorporates the use of visual structures (e.g., activity schedules and pictures for making choices, supporting transitions, and initiating interactions) and communication systems. For more information, visit http://www.pcdi.org.

TEACCH Services for Preschool Children

Division TEACCH (Treatment and Education of Autistic and Related Communication-Handicapped Children) is a statewide, state-funded, community-based program in North Carolina. Established in 1972, TEACCH is known in the United States and abroad for its assessment instruments, structured teaching model, and comprehensive and outstanding training for teachers and parents. For more information, visit http://www.teacch.com.

Summary

There are other effective public and private programs serving children with autism that offer parent and professional training. It is important to be aware of all options and maintain an open mind as you study them, but keep in mind the elements of effective programs and the needs of your child.

DEVELOP YOUR CHILD'S PROGRAM 8

One of your most difficult tasks is likely to involve making the many specific decisions required as you develop your child's intervention plan (IEP or IFSP). Decisions must be made that have no clear-cut answers. It is not always easy to pinpoint only a few essential goals. Which support services are essential? Which classroom will best meet your child's needs? There are so many issues and questions to consider. The administrative rule developed by your state educational agency for implementing IDEA (the public law briefly described in Chapter 5) will have a fairly straightforward process for assessing your child's educational needs and for developing the individual plan.

If you are lucky, your local program will have professionals with training and experience in providing services to children with autism. There will be teachers trained to understand how to match the accepted strategies to your child's various needs, and there will be at least one classroom that would make an appropriate placement. However, it will be much harder to make the best decisions if the staff of your local program has never served a child with autism and trained staff is not available for they may not recognize that modifications will be needed to accommodate your child's specific needs.

GUIDELINES FOR MAKING DECISIONS

In a paper titled, "The Criterion of the Least Dangerous Assumption," Donnellan (1984) suggested the following standard for making educational decisions: "in the absence of conclusive evidence, decisions ought to be based on assumptions which, *if incorrect*, will have the least dangerous effect on the likelihood that students will be able to function independently as adults" (p. 141).

The following eight guidelines for making decisions were developed with the above criterion in mind. In general, a cognitive/behavioral educational approach is based on these guidelines.

Guideline 1: The Autism Learning Style Provides the Foundation for All Decisions

The autism learning style (i.e., the information-processing differences) provides the foundation for assessing and understanding problems and for selecting teaching and intervention strategies. The critical goals that address the deficits of autism (see Figure 5) provide the basis for setting priorities—for deciding what to teach and how to teach it. The following two examples show how natural situations can be modified to accommodate learning differences and how the critical goals are given priority.

Tony's mother wants him to learn to brush his teeth and to do it independently so she will not have to be there to tell him each step. If Tony is to be totally independent, she must ask—and answer—the following questions before she begins to teach the skill. How will Tony know:

- When he needs to brush his teeth? (Will she tell him, or will he check his calendar?)
- What he needs to do to get ready to brush his teeth? (He will go to the bathroom to get his toothbrush and toothpaste.)
- How to brush his teeth? (She will show him each step, from taking the cap off of the toothpaste and putting toothpaste on the brush,

all the way through brushing and rinsing. He will need a checklist to show each step.)

- When he is finished? (His teeth are clean after brushing four times in each area of his mouth.)
- How to clean up? (Put the cap back on the tube, rinse the toothbrush, put both in their storage places, and so on. These steps may need to go on the checklist.)
- What to do next?

But, wait! If he is to be totally independent, Tony must be taught how to recognize and solve problems; for example, the toothpaste tube is empty, or his sister is at the sink when it is time for him to brush. He must be able to communicate a need for help, and be able to brush his teeth at home (in more than one bathroom) and in other bathrooms (if he stays overnight with Grandma, or if the family stays in a hotel).

Although this is a lot of planning, the child with the autism will not become independent unless we remember to teach all of these steps. But, he is learning a great deal in the process. In this single routine, he is achieving several critical goals. He is learning the language of all of the pieces of the routine; he is learning to use a calendar, follow a sequence of steps listed on a checklist so he won't need verbal prompts, and identify problems and communicate a need for help. He also is becoming more flexible.

The preschool children are at tables working with puzzles and pegs to strengthen their visual motor and perceptual skills. Tommy, who has autism and is good at pegs and puzzles, also is involved in the activity, but his priority is to increase his tolerance for sitting between two peers and strengthen the ability to express his needs. A classroom assistant is nearby helping another child while carefully watching Tommy for signs of stress. Just as his stress begins to increase, she says to him, "You look like you are tired and want to stop working." (She pauses briefly.) "You can tell me, 'Need break.'" She cues and assists him to use his communication system, and then says, "You need a break. Put in one more peg. Then you can take a break and jump on the trampoline." He quickly puts in a peg as she says, "Good! You are finished! You can go and jump."

She acknowledged and labeled his feelings and his need, gave him an opportunity to strengthen his communication skills, and briefly extended the amount of time he could work productively between two peers. The opportunity to jump on the trampoline—a favorite activity—reinforced his extra effort.

Guideline 2: Useful, Meaningful Skills Are Taught in Natural Settings

Teach useful, meaningful skills in natural, chronological and age-appropriate settings, so that from the beginning, the child learns what to do, where to do it, when to do it, and how to do it.

This principle has many applications, from deciding program placements to selecting teaching strategies. For example, those with autism need program placements in settings with other children of the same age who can serve as social and communication models. With an interpreter nearby, these children soon learn to watch and imitate peers. It also means that when new concepts or skills are introduced in a 1:1 or simulated situation, practice should be provided almost immediately in natural situations. Line drawings (or photos or words) to visualize the concept or sequence of steps provides a familiar reference in the different natural settings.

Guideline 3: Strategies and Materials Are as Natural as Possible

This principle is particularly important for children who learn and remember things exactly as taught and who often attach the wrong meanings to events. For example, if we want the child to do something independently, the child must be taught from the beginning to attend to the cues, prompts, and reinforcements that occur naturally in the environment. If we always tell the child each step of a task during instruction, the child will expect us to continue to tell each step of the task forever. The child builds *us* into the routine.

In another situation, if a child is taught that a picture of a cow *is* a cow, he likely will be unable to label that big four-legged creature in the pasture.

Guideline 4: *Therapies and Services Are Integrated to Support the Total Program*

There are several reasons to think seriously about this principle as we make decisions for children with autism. In the situation of speech-language therapy, if therapy always is provided in an isolated 1:1 situation, the child with autism is not likely to automatically begin to use the new skills out of the therapy room, in new situations, and with other people. But, if the speech-language pathologist introduces a new skill in a 1:1 setting, then demonstrates the strategies to school staff members and family, the child has opportunities to practice the skill in a variety of natural situations, all day, every day.

Guideline 5: *Visual Adaptations Support Learning and Independence in All Settings*

Visual adaptations and individualized support systems are available and used as needed to support learning and independence in all settings. This mean that all adults who spend time with the child at home and at school will serve as interpreters and guides who provide information visually in the form of checklists, calendars, and cue cards, so that the child can understand the environmental situation and the expectations of that situation.

It also means that the child must be taught several ways to communicate his needs and feelings. When a child can speak to express his needs and feelings, it is no guarantee that he will be able to use his speech effectively when under stress. We must provide backup systems that may involve pictures, written words, or gestures (such as pointing). It is not so important *how* the child communicates when stressed; what is important is that he *can* communicate *in some way*. The ability to communicate reliably in all situations, even with adaptations, will lead to greater independence.

Guideline 6: Strengths and Interests Are Developed and Used to Compensate for Deficits and to Increase Motivation

Developing and expanding the child's intense interests can enrich the child's life and provide a foundation for acceptance and friendships, as well as for vocational and leisure options as an adult. One child's interest in stereo speaker systems was used not only as a motivator, but he was taught to read, write, and spell while studying catalogs, magazine ads, and other material that featured speakers. For more examples of capitalizing on a child's interests, see Chapter 11.

Guideline 7: Program Goals, Activities, and Settings Are Balanced

In a balanced program, the child has many different kinds of opportunities to learn about the world, to participate in many ways with others, and to adapt to transitions and changes. Teaching strategies are integrated and adapted to a child's individual need at a specific time in a specific teaching situation. A balanced program also is safer; what if your child does not respond well to a single philosophy, strategy, or teaching format?

Children with autism have difficulty generalizing new skills to other situations. They are easily bored, and often are difficult to motivate. These problems can be addressed in the context of a balanced program.

 ◆ A few studies have shown that variety increases motivation for many children with autism.

Goals that are selected from three areas:
- Developmental goals (i.e., language, motor, social, and creative skills)
- Functional goals (i.e., skills and routines of daily life)
- Critical goals and pivotal skills that compensate for the deficits of autism (see Figure 5)

Chronological, age-appropriate activities that include:
- Instruction in 1:1, small-group, and large-group settings
- Opportunities for the child to initiate and take the lead as well as to follow adult-directed activities
- Work and play
- Seriousness and silliness
- Strenuous activity and quiet recovery time
- Opportunities to help others and to accept help from others
- Opportunities to work and play independently and cooperatively

Instructional strategies integrated and applied systematically:
- Behavioral principles to ensure that the child learns intended lessons
- Cognitive strategies to ensure that the child learns concepts and skills with accurate meaning and purpose attached
- Strategies modified to capitalize on the information-processing strengths and compensate for the processing deficits common to those with autism

FIGURE 9. Elements of a balanced program.

- When the child is exposed to a number of different settings and situations in which new skills are practiced, it takes less time to generalize skills.
- Many different skills and concepts can be taught at one time in the context of a broad and balanced range of natural, age-appropriate activities. Some of the components of a balanced program are highlighted in Figure 9.

A child benefits when the individualized program includes a balance of goals, activities, experiences, and strategies. It is dangerous to put too much emphasis on any one strategy goal or type of instruction.

Guideline 8: Expectations and Support Are Flexible and at a Level to Ensure Success Many Times Each Day to Maintain Motivation

For any child to maintain the motivation to try and to persist, the child must have a high rate of success. Just because a child with autism is able to do something one day does not mean that he will be able to do it the next day. Variable and inconsistent performance is common in autism. Therefore, we must adapt our expectations to match the child's ability to perform at any specific time.

If expectations and support are rigidly maintained even when the child is obviously stressed or "out of it," stress-related behavior problems increase and positive teaching time is lost. We always want to stop an activity in some positive way before the child falls apart. If we stop an activity after the child's behavior deteriorates, we are reinforcing and strengthening that negative behavior.

In Summary

These eight principles apply to all decision making for your child with autism. However, unique interests, strengths, past experiences, and patterns of development will demand highly individualized options and applications. This means that the enriched natural environment found in most early intervention, Head Start, and preschool programs can be an ideal placement for young children with autism, but only when the following two conditions are met:

1. There are enough staff members in a classroom so that someone is always available to keep the child alert and actively and productively engaged in group activities as well as 1:1 work and play sessions.

2. School staff members and parents are trained to understand the effects of autism on learning and behavior and to understand how to plan and deliver instruction to accommodate the autism learning style. (See pp. 99–102 for training resources.)

Now that you understand more about autism and have a decision-making principle and guidelines, it will be easier to define an appropriate program for your child. However, these decisions cannot be made until you have a decision about your highest priority long-term goal.

SELECT THE MAJOR LONG-TERM GOAL

What do you want for your child? This major long-term goal will determine the child's program and where the child is most likely to be when he is an adult. Parents ultimately must make this decision. But, the best decisions often are made with major input from a team of people with varied experiences. In fact, parents may support one long-term goal for educational planning while personally pursuing a different long-term goal. There are at least four possible long-term goals for the child with autism.

Option 1: To Cure Autism

This is the goal of most concern to many parents of younger children. Parents of older children have had enough experience to know that there are no real cures. Children with autism can learn many things and compensate for many of their deficits; but they are likely to continue to have at least some difficulty understanding and using social, communication, and language skills fluently; and they probably will continue to have difficulty planning, solving problems, and making decisions throughout their lives.

Option 2: To Make the Child "Look" Normal

Autism is a disorder of development—a neurobiological disorder that makes a major difference in how children with autism think about and respond to the world. There is enough evidence to know that many of the "autistic behaviors" serve an adaptive function. For example, when asked why they engage in repetitive behaviors, some individuals with autism have responded, "It relaxes me," or "It just happens when I don't pay attention to my body." One young man said, "When I look the most normal, I am the most uptight and stressed, for it takes so much energy to keep my body quiet that I have little time to focus on other things." There also is some evidence that these behaviors are a result of various types of seizure disorders.

This goal consumes so much time and energy for the family, staff members, and the student, that there is little left for learning more productive skills or having fun. When his son was nearing 18, one father said, "We wasted a lot of our son's precious time trying to cure his autism and make him look normal. He would be more independent now if our goal had been more realistic." We also know that as these children become more actively involved and productively engaged, the behaviors automatically decrease. Realistically, it is important to remember that we all have individual ways to deal with stress and boredom; these include drinking coffee, smoking, twisting strands of hair, or making repetitive movements with our feet or legs.

Option 3: To Get a High School Diploma

Some families feel it is very important for their child to graduate from high school with his peers. This goal is certainly within the potential of many higher functioning students if they have lots of support and if other critical goals can be met at the same time.

After Herculean efforts by family and school staff, one young man earned his diploma just like the others in his class, but he was very upset when he could not go on to college with his peers. He had only basic functional skills, and he had no idea how to manage his time, how to get help from others, how to manage his own stress, how to shop, or how to travel from one place to another.

Option 4: To Become as Independent as Possible

Perhaps this is the most realistic and valuable goal. With this goal, the child will work toward living a satisfying and productive life in the community as an adult. A goal such as this is wide open. It does not rule out academic study, nor does it rule out helping the individual fit into society.

Assuming that your choice will be for independence in the community, what then should we teach?

DEVELOP THE IEP OR IFSP

Each local school or agency will have a process for developing a child's Individualized Education Program (IEP) or Individual Family Service Plan (IFSP) that will fulfill the requirements of IDEA. The following discussion is arranged to follow a natural sequence of activities required for developing an individualized plan, although the process may vary somewhat among the various states and communities.

Assess Current Level of Functioning

The first step in developing the program plan is to determine your child's current level of functioning. What can your child do right now? This assessment is likely to involve some standardized testing by the speech-language pathologist and/or school psychologist. It also should involve a functional assessment to determine what your child does in the real environment. How does he let people know what he wants? What does he do at mealtime, at bedtime, at toilet time, at playtime, at home, in school, and in the community?

Parents have a major role in this assessment process. In the case of standardized tests, you most likely will be asked for information to help the evaluator communicate with your child, and for information about your child's preferences to determine which reinforcers are most effective. This is a critical issue if the goal of the assessment is to determine a child's actual abilities, rather than simply determine how your child responds to tests. Take a small bag of reinforcing toys or objects with you to give to the individual conducting the tests.

You may be asked to observe or review a videotape of the testing session to clarify the interpretations of some situations. As one psychologist concluded an assessment of play, she remarked that the child was amazingly capable of pretend play. The parents, who had observed the session, smiled as they answered, "Yes, it looks pretty creative. However, every time he plays with those particular toys, he does the very same things." In another situation, the child did not respond to many of the test questions even though the therapist had candy in view. The child's mother, who had been watching in the observation room, interrupted the session to give the therapist a small square of sheepskin to use as a reinforcer. As soon as the child saw the sheepskin, he became very alert and was able to answer many of the questions that previously he had failed.

Parents also are very involved in the functional assessment. They are an important source of information about their child's actual abilities in home and community situations. You may be given a questionnaire to complete that will help you organize your information prior to the interview. During the interview, an assessment coordinator will ask questions to clarify your thoughts and observations.

Select Priority Goals and Objectives

Once the assessment data is summarized, it is time to consider the information and determine your child's highest priority goals and objectives. Generally, the assessment coordinator presents the data to the IEP or IFSP team, and the plan is developed at the same meeting. This can be a very stressful situation for parents because there is so much new material to think about, and the process is unfamiliar. To alleviate this problem, ask to have the assessment results explained to you a few days before the planning meeting. This will give you time to ponder the information and prepare questions and ideas for goals.

The following question will help you and the team select the highest priority goals: *Which skills and concepts, if mastered now, would make the biggest difference in the child's ability to be more independent now and in the future?* The high-priority goals for the young child with autism will provide opportunities to achieve the critical goals (see Figure 5), especially those related to attending and involvement; understanding the language; increasing the ability to communicate, play, and interact with others; and increasing flexibility. The functional goals of dressing, toilet training, and other self-help skills also are fairly high priorities, both at home and at school.

The major consideration is that the goals should reflect a balance of skills so that all effort is not focused on only a single goal. Goals should be stated positively to reflect what the child will learn, rather than negatively to reflect what the child will stop doing. The objectives to achieve those goals will likely relate to those developmental concepts and skills that all young children must learn.

It is important to include a balance of the traditional preacademic and academic goals in the program for young children with autism. To assume that they will neither need nor be able to learn these skills will prevent these children from having opportunities to learn them. The potential for progress in academic areas will vary considerably, as will traditional academic progress. Traditional academic skills will provide opportunities to study about special interests and increase social and vocational options as these children grow older.

In most situations, the instructional strategies for achieving the goals and objectives are left for the professionals to determine. However, when autism is a factor, parents need to be more involved in these decisions to ensure that the strategies are those found to be most effective and that match the child's unique, individual processing style. The strategies also should be ones that the parents would be comfortable using at home to help the child transfer new skills from school to home, because it is important to use similar strategies in both settings.

Identify Support and Service Needs

The IEP or IFSP must include a list of the support services required for your child to make acceptable progress toward achieving the stated goals and objectives. The first four services listed below are basic and critical to ensure that your child will progress and achieve the stated goals. Additional services will depend on your child's specific needs. Support services include:

1. Training for parents and staff members to understand current information and strategies for teaching children with autism.

2. A staffing ratio of 1:1 to 1:3 for the very youngest child in a special class placement. If a child with autism is to be served in a general classroom setting with typically developing peers, generally there is a need for a classroom assistant. This assistant must be trained to understand autism, to serve as an interpreter, and to provide instruction in 1:1 work and play sessions and in small-group situations. The assistant needs to be in the classroom whenever your child is present, and must have time to consult and plan with the teacher. For more information about the interpreter's role, see pages 137–138.

3. Services of a speech-language pathologist and, if indicated, an augmentative communication specialist (see pp. 94–95).

4. Visual systems, including a daily calendar developed to match your child's individual developmental level, to provide information and prepare for changes and increasing independence. These systems must be available, modified as needed, and used systematically throughout each day.

5. Services of an occupational therapist trained in neural development. (See discussion of sensory integration therapy on p. 195).

6. Home support to help you make modifications to accommodate your child's needs while meeting the needs of the whole family. You also may need support to help your child to generalize new skills to other settings.

7. Adaptations to address safety needs (see pp. 122–124).

8. Transportation. Yes, this is even an option for young children with autism. I was amazed to see how quickly the 3-year-old children in my classes learned to carry their backpacks and travel to and from school on a big yellow school bus.

9. Other program accommodations. Often, other accommodations need to be included in the IEP or IFSP, because they are so critical for a child's progress. These include:

   ◆ A distraction-free area for 1:1 work and play sessions.

   ◆ Augmentative communication systems to help your child communicate before and during the time he is learning to communicate verbally. These may be picture systems (as in PECS), but also would include the use of gestures or possibly some type of computerized system.

   ◆ A positive behavior intervention plan based on a functional assessment of problems is a critical part of the IEP for some children.

   ◆ An extended school year often is needed for children with autism, for they have too much to learn to take 3 months off. A weekend and/or summer program need not duplicate the general school program, but it does provide a unique opportunity for strengthening and generalizing critical goals to many other settings and situations and with other people. It is important for these children to be kept alert and actively involved during the summer.

Be aware that program staff can refuse to provide some services or to use certain treatment strategies if there is no data to support their use with children who have autism. If you feel that those services are a necessity, see pages 125–129 about resolving conflicts.

Determine Class Placement

Placement in the least restrictive environment (LRE) is addressed in IDEA and explained on page 59.

Whether you are considering the local public program options, a private program model designed specifically for those with autism, or a home program, there are many questions to consider before making this critical decision for your child. The decision probably will involve a visit to several classrooms to understand the various options available.

Visiting a Classroom. When making a classroom visit, remember that the teacher is busy and may not have time to talk to you while the children are present. You are there to see how the environment is organized, how the teacher and staff members work with the children, and how the children function in that situation. This means that you will want to be as inconspicuous as possible. Make yourself small by sitting on the floor or in a small chair at the rear of the classroom. Scan the area and focus your attention on one or two children who have characteristics similar to your child's. See how the staff members respond to those children and how the teachers operate in the class. You may want to make some brief notes while you observe; when you return to your car, take time to clarify and enlarge those notes. If you visit several classrooms, it is difficult to keep track of the details of each.

Any time there are children together in a classroom, things may go wrong. This is especially true when there is a visitor. Things may get chaotic if a child has a tantrum or a classroom assistant is absent. Whatever the reason, the situation does provide an opportunity to see how a teacher handles the problem. But, don't be too quick to judge a teacher after only one visit; even the best teacher can have a bad day. A second visit will give you a chance for a different perspective. If you are seriously considering a specific classroom, make an appointment to meet the teacher when there would be time to talk. Time alone with the teacher will tell you a great deal, and perhaps will be the beginning of a positive and supportive relationship if your child ultimately is enrolled in the class.

Guidelines for Evaluating Placement Options. The following questions highlight most of the elements of an effective EI and preschool program for a child with autism. Many of these elements also are indicators of an effective program for any young child. You may find that some of these elements will have more relevance to your child than others. You also may find that there are important considerations that are not included. Your family values, philosophy, and resources, coupled with your child's specific needs, also will guide your decisions about placement.

Staff—Training and Organization

1. How does the teacher describe autism and the needs of children with autism? Does the description match the current understanding of autism?
2. Can the teacher describe the priorities of children with autism and the teaching strategies used to meet those needs?
3. Are there enough staff members so that there will always be someone available to serve as interpreter for your child and provide individualized work and play sessions?
4. Do assistants use strategies similar to those of the teacher? Is there a staff schedule posted or available so all personnel know which children they are to work with at various times, and what those children's priorities are? Is there a data-recording system in place to track children's progress and to record anecdotal notes to help interpret behavior?

Classroom Schedule

1. Is the classroom arranged in an orderly way so that children know where things are and where certain activities are carried out? For example, are there centers for music, books, blocks and toys, kitchen play, snack, work? Is there a small distraction-free area for 1:1 work and play sessions?

2. Are there any sensory factors (fan noises, flickering lights, crowding, clutter) that could overwhelm or distract your child? Are there safety factors to consider (e.g., unfenced play areas, busy streets)?

3. How much time would your child be involved in instruction? (How long is the instructional day? How much of that time would your child been actively involved in 1:1 work or play sessions, in small-group instruction, or in free play with an interpreter?) The primary consideration is that the child should be actively engaged most of the time.

Characteristics of Peers

1. Are there children of the same age who have good social and communication skills to serve as models and interactive play partners?

2. Are there peers with comparable motor skills? Although this may seem unimportant, I have been involved in several situations where a very active young child with autism was placed in a class with others in wheelchairs who had severe motor and health problems. Needless to say, the child with autism was frequently in trouble while having to wait for peers to be moved from one place to another.

Materials and Activities

1. Are children calm, busy, and involved; or is there a lot of down time when children are waiting and drifting? Are some children working independently? Are others working in groups of various sizes?

2. Is everyone doing the same things, in the same way, at the same time? Or, are children frequently grouped and regrouped and given optional tasks that allow some choice and individuality?

3. With what types of activities and materials are the children involved? Are they involved in rote or memorization tasks with pictures and flash cards? Or, are they interacting with real objects, real activities, and play with peers and teachers?

Teaching Strategies

1. What is the instructional emphasis? Is it on compliance? Rote responses? Or, is there an emphasis on teaching the child to be independent? Does the teacher provide a variety of visual systems to clarify expectations to support independence (cue cards, daily calendars, schedules, and checklists)?

2. What strategies would be used to help your child learn to develop trusting relationships and to communicate? Are the children using a variety of augmentative communication options? Are there many opportunities for children to initiate and take the lead in interactions in the context of structure play sessions and incidentally in natural situations?

3. Are the children successful most of the time? Are they given subtle gestural prompts (e.g., pointing or touching) to support correct responses and behavior? Are verbal and intrusive physical prompts avoided? Are errors dealt with in a positive way without reprimands?

4. How do staff members view and deal with problem behaviors? Are most behavior problems understood as a result of stress and an inability to communicate? What efforts or accommodations are used to prevent behavior problems (e.g., use of visual systems and rehearsal to prepare for changes and transitions)?

Home/School Involvement

1. Do staff members encourage collaboration and involve parents as an important source of information for solving problems? Are staff members open to new ideas and new strategies? Are you welcome to visit periodically? Are you encouraged to observe or help in the program?

2. Is training available to parents? What kind of training? Does it involve:

   * information specifically related to autism?

- strategies to help you cue, prompt, and reinforce your child?
- strategies for using visual systems?
- strategies to present or manage behavior problems?

3. Will the program staff members be available to help you set up and use the daily calendars and other visual systems at home? Will they help you resolve potential behavior problems at home?

One or two short observations will not provide enough time to observe all of these components. If a program includes most of these elements, and if the teacher is (or will be) trained to understand the needs of children with autism, it is likely that your child could be accommodated effectively.

Identify Safety Needs

Because children with autism are unaware of potentially dangerous situations, they present us with some very serious problems. They also have some unique abilities and disabilities that can cause harm, both to themselves and others. Some typical problems include those listed below.

- They have an unusual ability to open locks and childproof bottles. Some children are wanderers, and locks may delay them but not keep them from wandering. To understand the seriousness of this situation, read one mother's story on pages 123–124.
- They may smell, taste, and even eat things such as cigarette butts, items from the garbage, pieces of glass, and small tacks. Care must be taken to assure the safe storage of any potentially dangerous chemicals. Children with these problems will need instruction designed to teach them concepts such as what is and what is not food, and what is trash (or garbage), and where to put garbage when you find it. An occupational therapist is a resource if it appears that the problem is associated with sensory issues, such as odors, tastes, and textures. These children also need a most vigilant staff.

- Some children will respond unpredictably in an emergency. For example, those with extremely sensitive hearing may run and hide at the sound of alarms or sirens. Specific staff members must be assigned to be certain these students are escorted to safety in an emergency. Safety drills must be carefully planned and practiced many times in *all* settings.

- Other children may be attracted to windows (slamming into and even breaking glass), lights, fans, or high places. Screens or acrylic covers may be needed.

- These children do not automatically understand when they are sick or how to tell someone about pain. One 5-year-old boy in my class walked about all day with blisters on his heels. His mother discovered them at bedtime, after they had begun to bleed. Again, constant vigilance is necessary to watch for lethargy, flushed face, and any unusual change in behavior (such as banging ears, face, or head; stuffing things into the mouth, nose, or ears; and banging on the stomach). Much of the behavior associated with self-injury begins as a response to the pain of ear and sinus infections, migraine headaches, sore throats, or other medical problems. School staff members must report these behaviors to parents, including any pertinent information about the situation when it was first noticed. Parents and teachers need to develop a close and trusting relationship with the child's pediatrician to identify and treat any medical problems. Parents also may need to provide staff with information about common medical problems associated with autism.

One Mother's Story

Eileen Miller, the mother of Kim Miller (who made the drawings on pages 187–188), shared her solutions to one safety problem.

My daughter could only be safely contained in one room at a time. She choked on objects she put in her mouth, and poisoned herself with cleaners, medications, and hygiene products. She escaped from the house, ran in the road, and—because she had no attachment to us—she didn't come back. Unfortunately, childproof locks were no match for her. She could scale a gate across her doorway in less than a minute. We used combination padlocks, but she was able to crack the code in 3 days. We changed the code, she cracked it again. This is finally how we kept her in her room:

We took the bedroom door to [a shop that specialized in making custom doors]. We asked to have the door split in half. They thought we were crazy. When we brought the door home, we determined that the upper half could be a hazard, so we stored it. New hinges were installed. We reversed the doorknob so that the locking mechanism was on the outside. Then we went to Radio Shack and found a window/door alarm. After it was installed, any jolt or motion of the door opening would sound the alarm and we would know when she was slipping out.

There are a number of safety advantages to this method:

- Parents can glance over the door at any time and check on the child.
- The sound of the alarm can be used as a teaching tool—a cue to the child to ask permission to leave.
- The alarm gives the parents a head start to intercept before the child is missing.

No safety alarm is foolproof or a replacement for adult supervision; but in the exceptional case of a child with autism bent on escaping at all costs, it does give the parent a tool to take control of an out-of-control situation.

Parents die a little more inside each time they find out that they are unable to keep their child safe. Each incident is compounding to the point that you wonder when you will either have to give up your child to the professionals to keep her safe, or find the child injured or worse.

Funds for alarms might be available to parents through Supplemental Social Security Income (SSI) or from community organizations interested in helping those with disabilities.

HOME/SCHOOL CONFLICTS

Relationships between families and school personnel can be fragile. Sometimes conflicts occur during the IEP or IFSP development process, especially when the child has autism. Parents tend to be more assertive when they are informed about autism, understand their child's basic needs, and realize that they must be their child's lifelong advocate.

Although the law specifies that every child should have a free and *appropriate* program, there is no clear definition of an appropriate program for children with autism. The law specifics that funding issues should not determine the child's program plan. Rather, it is the child's needs that determine an appropriate program; it is the child's needs that determine the type and intensity of the program, the type and intensity of therapies, and the type of classroom placement. The needs of a child with autism are identified by a thorough assessment conducted by—or at least interpreted by—a professional with knowledge and experience of autism (see pp. 58–59).

Most problems occur when parents feel that the program offered or provided by their local school district is not adequate or appropriate for their child, and they ask the district administrators:

- to fund a specific model to be implemented at school, at home, or in both settings;
- to increase the services for their child, such as the number of staff, extent of staff training, or hours of in-class or therapy time; and
- to consider a particular school placement that they feel is less restrictive.

Problems can be complicated if local school administrators:

- feel that the program they provide will fit every child with disabilities and they are unable to see that those with autism need some specific individualized accommodations;
- have not specifically defined or clarified their model of services for children with autism, nor have data to support the validity of their model for those with autism;
- have developed a service model that is limited to a self-contained class for all children with the diagnosis of autism regardless of the child's level of functioning and individual need; and
- do not philosophically agree with the specific program model requested by parents.

In these or similar situations, parents must give careful thought and weigh their options. It is true that the child needs appropriate services as early as possible, and although a few months may not make a significant difference, a year might. But, before making any decisions, parents need to adhere to the following.

- Understand the provisions of the law. IDEA spells out the responsibilities of the school district, and it provides a basic process for resolving disagreements about a child's program. This resolution process includes mediation and other options.
- Talk to well-informed parents who have been effective in obtaining an appropriate program for their child. If possible, get advice from a professional educator who is not employed by your district, but who understands the needs of those with autism.
- Keep a record of all contacts, meetings, and phone calls with district personnel that are related to efforts to obtain changes in a child's program. Include dates, the name or names of those involved, and a summary of the discussion. Keep copies of all correspondence, including letters sent and received. Assume that if a situation cannot be substantiated, it is likely to be treated as if it didn't happen.

- Request an independent assessment of the child's needs from an evaluator who is not a member of the district staff. IDEA specifies that the district is responsible for funding such an evaluation.
- Seek advice from an expert in the education of those with autism, an attorney who understands and has experience with special education law, and from parents who have successfully or unsuccessfully pressed their case in court. It also is helpful to talk with parents who have taken their child out of the school program and provided a home program.
- Take an advocate to meetings (see pp. 60–61).

After studying the options, parents must do what seems best for their child and their whole family. Parents do have the long-term responsibility to be their child's advocate.

If parents have the resources, they may decide to implement a specific educational model in their home at their own expense, or they may continue to press the district for all or part of the cost. If families make the decision to take their child out of the local school and to implement an intensive program, their primary goal is most likely to prepare their child to eventually re-enter the local general education program.

If the ultimate goal is to have the child integrated into the regular program with typically developing peers, some parents choose to maintain contact with the staff members of their local school system. In fact, parents may ask the local teacher and/or speech-language pathologist to visit the home periodically to see how the child responds to the program and to help evaluate the child's progress. If the family and the school staff members can remain partners, it will be easier for everyone when the child is ready to transition back into the local program.

It is important to know that most professionals are dedicated to the children they serve and work hard to provide a most appropriate program. If there comes a time when you must press to ensure the best for your child, be cautious. Do not personally alienate your local school staff members, for most likely you will need to work with them at some point in the future.

One mother who has an older child with autism offered the following information that she wished she had known earlier:

- *Use the correct terminology.* When speaking about your child's service needs, use the term *appropriate*. Do not use the terms *optimal* or *best*; the district is required only to provide an appropriate program.

- *Talk to the people in charge.* If you are unhappy with your child's program and want to make basic or important changes in the level or type of services, talk to the director of special education of your local school district. Special services often are provided by subcontractors, but the local school district is legally responsible for your child's program.

- *Some people at the IEP meetings cannot advocate for your child.* Even when a teacher or therapist is supportive and works well with your child, that person is not free to speak out against district policy in a public situation.

- *Service providers are not all equally skilled.* After you are familiar with autism and your child's rights, identify local professionals who know the most about autism—people who have demonstrated success in addressing the needs of those children. Keep a list of teachers, speech therapists, occupational therapists, and others—those who may be employed by the district as well as those who are independent of the local district. These are the people you will turn to for advice or to provide an independent assessment.

- *Special education was never intended to be a place.* Rather, special education is a set of individualized services to address a wide range of needs. These individualized services must be at a meaningful level of intensity to ensure that the child is successful in the least restrictive environment. The services follow the child; the child does not go to the services.

- *Students in special education are entitled to progress reports.* If the children in the general school program get quarterly progress reports, your child also should get a quarterly report. This report should include a review of the child's progress and a projection to determine whether your child will achieve IEP goals at the appropriate time. If progress is not at an acceptable rate, the services should be adapted to increase the child's rate of learning.
- *Children who exhibit problem behaviors have rights.* When a behavioral crisis is related to a child's disability, as in autism, the district personnel cannot simply change his placement (i.e., expel the child or move him to a more restrictive setting). Rather, a functional analysis of the problem must be conducted and a positive behavior intervention plan to prevent recurring problems must be developed and implemented.

ESTABLISH POSITIVE RELATIONSHIPS

It is to your child's advantage for you to develop a positive working relationship with the special education director or EI supervisor. This person is responsible for the quality of the program and for ensuring that the IEP or IFSP is implemented as agreed. It also is important to develop trusting relationships with members of your child's support team, especially the teachers and therapists who work directly with your child. They need to know you are interested and want to be actively involved. Although they are very busy, generally they welcome interested parents as long as those parents do not intrude on their time with other children during the school day. There are many ways to strengthen these relationships:

- Make periodic appointments after the children leave.
- Acknowledge their efforts. Let them know when your child has learned something new.
- Request information. Ask them to show you how they deal with a specific problem.

- Occasionally ask whether they would like to see an article or book on autism you have just finished reading. Perhaps you may set a time to discuss issues and new strategies.
- Ask the team members for short IEP review meetings every few weeks to review, predict, and prevent learning or behavior problems.
- Be sensitive about the professionals' time. They have many children to think about.
- Although you would not take a teacher's time during classroom teaching time, it is important that you and the teacher share information that may affect your child's behavior during the day. For example, if informed immediately that your child has a sore arm because of a vaccination, the teacher can be sensitive to any changes in behavior, a fever, and a need to sleep. If the teacher informs you that your child was upset at school for some reason, you will know how to respond to his behavior that evening. A small notebook that can be tucked into your child's backpack and carried to and from school each day is a valuable tool. It takes only a few minutes to jot significant information into the book, and it provides an opportunity to share little anecdotes and insights about your child's behavior.

Parents need to be reassured that most teachers and therapists are extremely conscientious and hard working. They truly want to do all they can to help a child and work with the family. However, if conflicts do occur, review the information on pages 125–129.

PART IV
BASIC STRATEGIES

STRATEGIES FOR PREVENTING PROBLEM BEHAVIORS

9

A lthough behavior is influenced by many things, our actions largely are determined by our understanding or perspective of a situation. We generally believe that everyone operates from our point of view. For example, when we considered most problem behavior as willful and intentional, we applied the principles of punishment to eliminate it. As a result, many people with autism spent their lives in institutions under restraint and drugged. Now we know that people do have different perspectives that result from past experiences and how they process the information from those experiences. When Dr. Wing (1980) said that to help those with autism we must look at the situation from their perspective (see p. 17), she implied that their perspective was much different than ours. And so it is. To figure out the point of view of a child with autism, we must have a broader understanding of behavior.

UNDERSTANDING BEHAVIOR

Studies of behavior have determined that there are at least four basic concepts to consider when trying to understand an individual's behavior:

1. Behavior is communication—a logical response to a current situation and an effort to regulate conditions that do not match needs. For example, a hungry infant cries—a reflexive, unintentional act.

The infant's behavior signals a need, but the need must be interpreted by others, usually the parents.

2. Behavior is a logical response to the environment in which it was first learned. If that same infant doesn't learn to communicate more intentionally and clearly, he will continue to cry when he is hungry, and probably to get other needs met as well. Perhaps the child's parents would be able to tolerate this because they had learned to understand the meaning of that cry. As the infant grew up, life would become more difficult when the parents are not around. Others might interpret the crying as a form of laziness or attention seeking, and would ignore or attempt to eliminate it. When the history of a behavior is lost, problem behaviors occur and escalate because we do not have the information to interpret the meaning accurately and respond appropriately.

3. Behavior is an attempt of the brain to keep itself stimulated or in equilibrium. Repetitive and stereotypic movements most often occur when the individual is bored, anxious, or overstimulated. The behaviors simply are more intense versions of our own nervous habits.

4. Behavior is an outward expression of an inward state. Fear, worry, stress, fatigue, and illness—anything from a headache to seizure activity—can affect behavior by decreasing tolerance and control. Generally, problem behaviors that occur at these times are reflexive in nature and difficult to interpret. Although undiagnosed seizure activity is beyond personal control, it should be considered in an assessment of problem behavior.

This broader perspective of behavior removes much of the stigma from those with autism, who understand the world differently. The person is no longer the problem; those with autism have problems, but few logical solutions. If there are logical solutions to these problems, what are they?

1. If the environment does not make sense, we modify the environment to make more sense.
2. If the child lacks skills to express feelings and needs and to seek help, we teach those skills.
3. If there is a medical problem, we seek help to treat the problem.
4. If the child needs a way to release tension and energy, we teach him ways to relax and how to ask for a break.
5. Perhaps the most important thing we can do for the child is to interpret his need, acknowledge his message, and provide support to resolve his problem.

This all sounds great, but how do you interpret the meanings of behavior? First, we must examine the effects of stress.

THE EFFECTS OF STRESS ON BEHAVIOR

All of us—including those with autism—have stress at some time during each and every day. In fact, if we had no stress, we would never get anything done. If one draws a line to represent the changing levels of stress that occur throughout the day, it would look somewhat like the line in Figure 10. There would be periods of barely fluctuating stress, and periods of ups and downs as problems arise and are resolved.

Our individual profiles of stress will look much the same; although some will have quick and sharp highs and lows, some will show extremes of highs and lows, and others will show a slow buildup of stress. If a small section of the profile is enlarged to examine a single episode of intense stress that included a crisis situation, a predictable profile emerges. The profile of this episode is typical of all crises.

Notice that each episode can be divided into four stages. Stage 1 illustrates the beginning and buildup of stress. If problems build and continue to occur with no solutions in sight, the stress level rises until

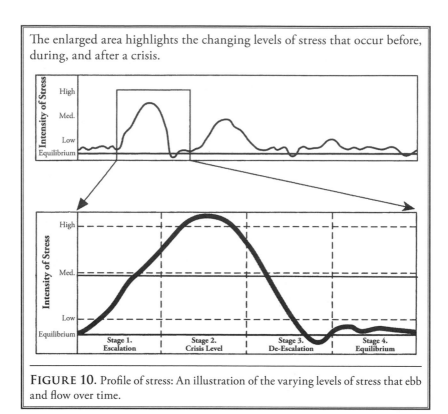

The enlarged area highlights the changing levels of stress that occur before, during, and after a crisis.

FIGURE 10. Profile of stress: An illustration of the varying levels of stress that ebb and flow over time.

it peaks and an emotional crisis is at hand at Stage 2. At that point, an individual knows he should do something, but doesn't know what to do or how to do it. If the pressure remains or is increased, the individual will blow up, swear, take off, or use some method to release the pressure.

As stress begins to diminish (as at Stage 3), the individual feels exhausted and spent, and sometimes has difficulty getting back to a productive stage. In fact, if the stress had been building for a long time and the crisis took a good bit of energy, the individual is so vulnerable that even a small problem could cause a rapid increase in stress, resulting in another crisis. But, once the individual feels calm, energy returns. Once a course of action is clear, the person will feel alert, ready to take on problems and be productive again, as at Stage 4.

This view of the levels of stress is the basis for understanding when and how to match our interventions to a child's need; for a child's behavior looks different at each stage, and his need is different at each stage.

AN UNDERLYING PRINCIPLE

Now that we have a better understanding of behavior, I want to emphasize the following principle developed from my many years of experience with many individuals with autism:

> I believe that it is unethical and unproductive to punish behavior that occurs as a result of confusion, anxiety, panic, or the lack of skill and ability to ask for clarification, assistance, or basic needs. The most powerful behavior management strategies are those that prevent problems or do not make problems worse.

STRATEGIES AND SUPPORT SYSTEMS

Now we must identify effective strategies and support systems to prevent and manage problem behaviors. The most critical need of each individual who cannot make sense of the environment is to have an interpreter or a guide. Who are the interpreters and what will they do?

The Interpreter—Provider of Critical Support

Parents, teachers, teaching assistants, mentors, peers, brothers and sisters, or any person in a support role who knows the child well, is—or can be—an interpreter. Sometimes a person is hired to interpret in a specific setting. Therefore, the term *interpreter*, as used in the remainder of this book, refers to any person who has responsibility for the individual with autism at any give time or place. At home or at school, it will be important to specify who the interpreter will be. Otherwise, there may be times when no one is monitoring. Lack of monitoring is not only unsafe, but leaves the child without someone to interpret when interpretation is needed—much like the situation of those who are blind or unable to hear.

What Does the Interpreter Do? Paraphrasing Webster's definition, an interpreter/guide is one who restates in clear language to convey meaning, one who assigns meaning to events, actions, or intentions, and shows the way. An interpreter/guide highlights critical information and directs efforts.

If the child with autism is to become as independent as possible in the natural environment, initially the child will need someone in every setting and situation who can serve in the role of interpreter. This means that one person in every setting will be assigned to be alert to the things, people, and events present in a situation that are likely to be confusing to the child with autism. Then the interpreter provides information so the child can learn from the situation and know what to do.

This does *not* mean that the interpreter must always stay beside the child and tell the child everything to do; nor does it mean that the interpreter smooths the way to the extent that the child never has to learn how to deal with problems. Rather, the interpreter can be involved with other people and activities while being in the same general area with the child. While attending to other things, the interpreter can scan the area and watch for signals that the child is becoming or may become confused and anxious. It is a role much like that of a mother who seemingly "has eyes in the back of her head."

The need for interpreters is most urgent in early childhood if the child is to learn to make sense of the environment. The need also is critical in highly stressful situations throughout the lifespan—during illnesses and major life transitions such as moving to a new home, changing jobs, or losing close and trusted family members and friends. As skills and independence grow, the need for an interpreter changes or varies.

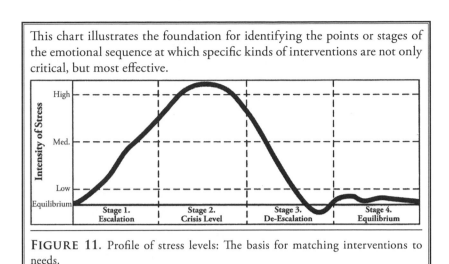

This chart illustrates the foundation for identifying the points or stages of the emotional sequence at which specific kinds of interventions are not only critical, but most effective.

FIGURE 11. Profile of stress levels: The basis for matching interventions to needs.

Matching Intervention to Needs

In Figure 11, note that behavior changes as a child's level of stress intensifies at each stage, indicating that the child's needs will change as well. The interpreter's goal and role also must change at each stage to match the child's need.

Interpreters are both proactive, thinking ahead to prevent problems; and reactive, responding to current problems. In general, they have four major goals that correspond to the four stages of stress.

Stage 1. Stress is escalating and behavior increases in intensity
Interpreter's goal: To defuse stress to avoid the crisis
Interpreter's tasks:
1. Identify the *subtle* behavior that signals stress (restlessness, pushing away, rocking, flushed face, change in breathing, or other behaviors).
2. Interpret the message.
3. Acknowledge the problem and suggest a solution (e.g., say to the child, "Jimmy moved his chair too close. You can tell him, 'Move over.'").

4. Provide support to resolve the problem to avoid the crisis. (Gently guide the child to place his hands on Jimmy's arm, and say for him, "Move over.")

Stage 2. Crisis level; child is highly vulnerable or out of control
Interpreter's goal: To keep people safe
Interpreter's tasks:
1. If there is time, cue the child to go to his quiet area. If there is no time and potential exists for others to get hurt, cue them to leave the area.
2. If possible, solve the problem quickly to relieve the stress.
3. Stay calm, and remove demands. Back away to give the child a bit of space. Stop talking. Remember that the child is in a panic mode and unable to think. Further pressure to perform or to make a choice will increase his panic, escalating to a crisis.
4. Keep people safe. To prevent damage or injury during a crisis, one may need to use gentle but firm restraint of some kind. *This would be a crisis procedure, not an intervention.* An intervention teaches the child a skill for solving or dealing with the problem the next time it occurs. A child who is out of control and in a crisis is not able to think and not able to learn; so this is not a teaching time. A note of caution: Restraint should not become a regular procedure. If a child is regularly in crisis, ask for a functional assessment of the problem in order to develop a positive behavior intervention plan that addresses the child's true needs. If there is a potential for injury, family and staff members should be trained in nonaversive crisis management procedures.

Stage 3. Calming, de-escalating behavior
Interpreter's goal: To support recovery and help the child to re-engage in ongoing activity
Interpreter's tasks:
1. Remain nearby, calm, and quiet. Do not make demands.

2. As the child begins to calm (even if it is only to stop screaming to take a deep breath), quietly say, "Good! You can relax yourself," or, "It will be OK."

3. When the child is totally calm, prepare him for the next activity ("When the timer rings, it will be time to _____."). Support with a visual cue card or object to represent the next activity or to check the child's calendar.

Stage 4. Calm and stable behavior; stage of equilibrium
Interpreter's goals:

1. To maintain an optimum level of stress; that is, enough stress to maintain alertness, but not so much to lose control.

2. To teach new skills. Only when the child is operating at this stage of equilibrium is he relaxed and alert enough to be open to teaching and available for learning.

Interpreter's tasks:

1. Predict and prevent potential problems by preparing the child for new or changing situations and expectations.

2. Monitor the child's level of stress. If unexpected problems occur, provide support to resolve them quickly to defuse stress and prevent a crisis.

3. Teach new skills to prevent recurring problems (e.g., to request help; to indicate need for a break; relaxation skills).

4. Continually evaluate and refine the organization of space and materials, routines and activities, schedules, and expectations to match a child's changing needs.

5. Clarify the environment and the expectations of people in that environment so the child can learn from the natural activities of the day.

Preventing Problems

The interpreter's primary or most important role is to function pro-actively—to think ahead and predict and prevent potential problem situations. This is a two-step process:

1. Identify potential problem situations.
2. Modify the situation or prepare the child before he is expected to participate in a difficult situation.

Typical Problem Situations. Situations that seem ordinary and tolerable to us can be overwhelming to those with autism. As one understands the nature and effects of the information-processing style common in autism (see pp. 20–29), it is fairly easy to predict which situations will be stressful for any individual child. Yes, problems are predictable; they are likely to occur whenever the child misunderstands or misinterprets a situation or is overwhelmed by sensory stimulation. You can predict that your child will experience escalating confusion, anxiety, and stress in the following situations:

1. *When a critical bit of information is missing or misunderstood and the individual is unable to ask for clarification.* For example, when the individual:
   - does not know that he lacks the information,
   - does not understand that he can ask for information, or
   - does not know how to ask questions to clarify the situation.

   Stress will escalate faster if the child knows he is to do something, but it is not clear about some small aspect of the situation (e.g., what, when, where, how, how much, how long, or what next).

2. *In situations with people.* People provide a great deal of confusing stimulation when:
   - they make too much noise; they have harsh or shrill voices;

- too many people speak at one time; they use too many words;
- people get too close; they give off odors; they touch unexpectedly;
- they wave their hand about, and their facial expressions change; or
- they criticize, make demands, repeat requests, and rush about.

If the child already is confused and people push for a response or talk louder, or several people try to help and talk at the same time or get too close, a crisis is likely to occur.

3. *When something is new or changed, or when something is added or missing.* For example:
   - when new activities, materials, toys, or new foods are introduced;
   - when a familiar schedule or routine is changed;
   - when new people are present (a substitute teacher, babysitter, neighbor);
   - when a familiar person or familiar object is missing (a parent or teacher, a favorite comfort object); or
   - when in a new or unfamiliar location or setting.

4. *During interruptions* (e.g., not being allowed to finish an activity or complete a routine) *and transitions* (e.g., going to and from meals or getting ready to go to and from home to the store). During these times, there is apt to be more noise, movement, and general stimulation, and the child is unsure about what he should be doing.

5. *When bored or required to wait.* You can predict that a child will become bored or stressed when required to:
   - do the same thing for too many times in a row,

- do things that have no obvious meaning,
- wait for a period of time with nothing to do,
- do too easy a task over and over, or
- wait while his mother talks to a friend.

The child with autism already is confused about time and time concepts. How will he know when the boring work or the waiting time will end?

6. *When feeling ill or when injured.* There is considerable evidence that for most of us, stress and anxiety increase during these times when tolerance is low. The child with autism, who cannot tell people that he is ill or in pain, does not understand if or when these bad feelings will ever go away. It is no wonder that we see evidence of self-abuse and other unexpected behavior at these times.

If you can commit this list to memory, you automatically can check it so you can prepare your child to participate in new or changing situations. This list also can help you determine the cause of increasingly stressful behavior.

Prevent Stressful Situations

Many of these predictable problems can be prevented—but how? Let's imagine that you are to have visitors from Mongolia and there is no interpreter available. Because you cannot assume that these people from Mongolia will know anything about our culture or our language, what will you do? How will you help them feel comfortable in this very different culture?

First, you will show respect, for you know that they have strengths and abilities that can be used to help them understand, but it will be up to you to figure out how to clarify things. You will need to serve as the interpreter.

Most likely you will find out as much as you can about the Mongolian culture and try to learn a few critical words of the language even before the visitors arrive. Then you will begin to anticipate potential problems and plan ahead to prevent those problems. What will they need to know? How will you give them information? How can you help them relax? Most likely, you would:

- Speak softly and clearly, and use gestures to clarify the words.
- Make information visual and permanent for later reference. You would draw pictures, maps, charts, and checklists.
- Organize space and events to show where certain things will occur.
- Make a list or calendar to show when things will occur, and alter the list to show any changes.
- Give the visitors a tour of the space. Show them where things are and demonstrate how things work. Prepare a checklist with pictures for the visitors to follow during the demonstration.
- Use only critical words, and try to have fun.

These are the very strategies that will be helpful in working with those with autism who do not automatically learn to understand their own culture.

Clarify Expectations With Visual Systems

We all need and use visual information systems. Our lives would be chaotic if we did not use calendars, appointment books, "to do" lists, road signs, white and yellow lines on the highways, areas for lining up in banks and airports, base lines, lane lines, yard lines in athletics, and directions on packaged foods, pesticides, and medications. If these systems are so important to those of us who can make sense of the things we see and hear, how much more important are they to those who have trouble processing the things they hear?

Visual information systems are powerful behavior prevention and management tools for those with autism. They provide a continuing reference so the child understands what is going to happen and what he is

ILLUSTRATION 1. This cue card reminds the child where he can go to relax. It is introduced as he is being taught to recognize his own stress and to ask for and take a break to recover.

to do. Visual systems are used to prepare these children for changes and for new activities, people, and settings.

- Visual systems are used to defuse stress at Stage 1. A simple cue card can clarify what to do right now to solve a problem (e.g., a card with printed words, "First, coat. Then outside.").

- At Stage 2, a quick line drawing of a child's rocking chair could cue a very tense child to go to the chair and rock to release tension, thus breaking the chain of escalation. (See Illustration 1.)

- At Stage 3, setting a timer could prepare the child to re-engage in the next activity.

- During the Stage 4 level of stress, calendars provide information so the child knows when things will occur (see Illustrations 2 and 3). Checklists are used to clarify the order for completing a task or to understand that the shopping trip will involve several different stops.

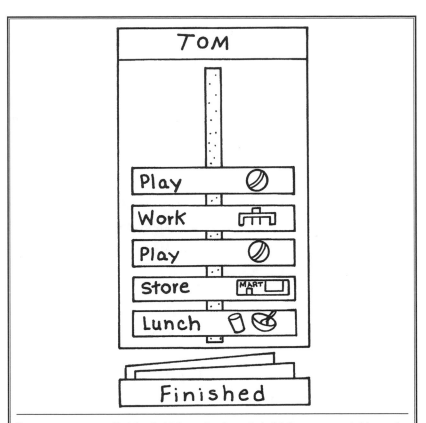

ILLUSTRATION 2. This half-day calendar is helpful for younger children who have difficulty envisioning time.

ILLUSTRATION 3. A weekly calendar is important for the child who becomes confused about no school on the weekends.

It is nothing short of amazing to see how much more independent and relaxed children become when we make a point of ensuring that they have the information they need. One young boy who could not stay in the appropriate classroom area quit wandering about after he was taught to understand the meaning of the big red stop sign propped on a small chair placed in his path. (For additional examples, see Chapter 10.)

THE PROCESS FOR DEFUSING STRESS

No matter how committed, we simply cannot predict and prevent all problems. In fact, it would not be productive for the interpreter to be so helpful and solicitous that the child never had to encounter a problem. If the child is to become more competent and independent, he needs to be taught to identify and resolve problems. However, without the support of interpreters, the child's stress level is likely to escalate to a crisis situation in which learning cannot take place. To defuse stress, avoid a crisis, and return to equilibrium—the stage at which the child can learn efficiently and behave effectively—interpreters must understand how to:

1. identify the earliest behavioral signs of stress that signal a need to communicate;
2. identify the cause of the problem—the communicative function of the behavior (i.e., identify the child's need); and
3. provide visual information and support to help solve the problem (meet the child's need).

Identify the Early Signals of a Problem

How will the interpreter know when stress is increasing? Most interpreters already know their child very well. They will notice the variations of expression and behavior that occur throughout the day. We have learned that these behaviors signal a need. But, because the child cannot express the need in conventional ways, it is up to us to interpret the need and help the child solve the problem. If the earliest signals are not recognized and the problems resolved in a timely way, stress will increase. Generally, as stress increases, the intensity of the behavior signals increases and chains of escalating behavior develop.

As an example of this escalating chain of behavior, let me tell you about my experience with one little boy. For more than 20 minutes, Barry had been working with his teacher on a variety of table tasks. As I observed, he began to get *restless* (squirming, stretching). When his teacher placed a new task before him on the table Barry *gently pushed the materials away*. As the teacher pulled the block task closer, he said harshly, "Hands down!" and continued to tell Barry what to do. Barry *threw one of the blocks on the floor*. The teacher said, "Pick up the block." Barry got down and picked up the block, but *stayed under the table and refused to get out*. This situation escalated to a major *screaming and kicking tantrum* as the teacher continued to make demands. Never once did he acknowledge Barry's early and very appropriate attempts to communicate that he was tired and needed a break.

The critical issue, then, is to identify the smallest signals of stress, and intervene before the stress increases to trigger more intense behavior. You may already know your child's early subtle signals of stress. They probably fall into the following categories:

1. Physical signs of confusion, frustration, anxiety, or fatigue: flashing, yawning, stretching, or changes in breathing patterns.
2. Repetitive/stereotypic verbal or motor actions: rocking, finger flicking, or repetitive questions often related to time and events.
3. Disorganized behavior: random, frantic, or compulsive behavior (dashing about, picking up or putting down an object). As one little boy dashed around and around the gym, he kicked the teacher's leg each time he passed. Later it was interpreted to mean that he wanted to play with the teacher, but he didn't know how to ask. When he was taught to touch the teacher's arm to get her attention, the child stopped the kicking behavior.

4. Signs of apathy, lack of motivation, or withdrawal: covering ears, scooting down in the chair, closing eyes, putting head down on table, limpness, or turning away.

5. Signs of resistance (apparent noncompliance): Dropping to the floor, pulling away, running away, or pushing or throwing materials away.

6. Emotional outbursts that don't fit the situation: Giggling and laughing when someone is hurt, shouting out, and so on. One child would stand on his desk and shout, "Mrs. Brown, this is no laughing matter!" It was later discovered to mean that he had about all the confusion he could handle during transitions.

7. Self-injury: biting wrist, slapping or banging face or head.

8. Apparent aggression: pinching, scratching, hitting, or kicking.

We know that when a child has a problem and has no alternative solutions, stress will escalate. When our stress gets too high and we have no solutions, we sometimes act reflexively. We may fidget, swear, pound the table, or throw something. So, too, the child with autism acts reflexively when faced with an overwhelming problem. These last-straw behaviors generally are intense, but not done intentionally to hurt anyone. Therefore, it is critically important to identify the earliest signals of the problem, interpret the need (or communicative intent), and help the child resolve the problem quickly.

Interpret the Cause of Increasing Stress

Once the earliest signals are identified, remember the list of situations that lead to problems (see pp. 142–144). Then ask yourself, from the child's perspective at this moment, why is this happening?

- What has the child misunderstood?
- What is unclear? What is not visually clear?
- What is new or changed or missing?

- What could be overwhelming? Noise from a fan? People talking outside the door? Crowding? Is the work to hard or too easy? Has the child been sitting too long?
- Is the child bored? Tired? Ill? Could it be seizure activity?
- Does the child have a way to communicate the problem? What would the child say right now, if he could? ("I need to move!"; "That noise is driving me crazy!"; "I don't understand"; or, perhaps, "You smell like garlic, and it makes me feel sick.")

Provide Assistance to Resolve the Problem

Once the problem is identified, clarify it by giving your child information in an organized and meaningful verbal and visual format, as described and illustrated on pages 145–148. Then provide whatever support is needed to involve the child in solving the problem. The following suggestions can help your child learn the language of the situation and feel accepted and valuable.

1. Listen to what the child says and does; reflect his meaning and feelings; and then tell him what to do. For example:
   - Say, "You are thirsty and want a drink." (Pause for a brief acknowledgment or response.) "You can tell me, 'Drink.'" Then provide assistance to help the child use his communication system, and quickly give him a drink.
   - Say, "You are tired and want to stop working. Do one more. Then you can get down and play."

2. Be supportive. Make calm statements to provide reassurance ("It will be OK"; "You will be able to ____"; "I will help you").

If your child often is stressed or stress builds quickly to Stage 3 proportions, relaxation training may be a high priority.

STRATEGIES FOR GIVING DIRECTIONS

We can prevent behavior problems by making sure that our verbal directions are clear and understandable. The following strategies are helpful for all children, but critical for those with autism.

Teach the Meaning of New Directions

If a child is to follow a direction, he must be taught the meaning of the words in a direction.

1. Get the child's attention before giving any direction.
   - Get close to the child and move down to the child's eye level.
   - Perhaps hold the child's hands or gently but firmly touch his shoulder while saying his name.
   - Pause briefly to give the child a chance to respond. Wait quietly for several seconds until the child acknowledges you in some way (looks at you quickly, relaxes, or comes nearer).

2. Quickly state the direction as clearly as possible (see pp. 153–157).
3. Be ready and prepared to provide assistance to ensure that the child follows the direction quickly and fluently.
4. Express pleasure, and have something pleasurable begin as soon as the child follows the direction. For example, when you have the child's attention, say, "Dinner is ready. Come to the table." Guide the child to the table and into the chair. As the child sits, be enthusiastic (but not overpowering) as you say, "Good boy! You came to the table. Here is an olive to eat" (assuming that olives are a favorite food!).

A Few Words About Eye Contact

There is no doubt that eye contact is an important social skill, so let us teach it in the context of a social interaction or in an interactive play session. However, there is no guarantee that children with autism understand better when they look into your eyes. In fact, there is some evidence that making direct eye contact may be overstimulating and stressful for at least some of these children. There also is some evidence that peripheral vision is better than direct vision for some children with autism.

If the child glances quickly to acknowledge your presence and stays quietly near you, he probably is attending and will comply if he knows exactly what to do. Our role is to teach him what the words mean, give him visual cues, demonstrate, or give other physical and visual prompts.

Give Clear Directions

When giving directions, we must use language clearly and precisely. If we want these children to understand the language of their culture, they must hear it correctly. They will not be able to automatically analyze the words and figure out your unspoken meaning as other children do. Remember that you are serving as a language model.

1. Speak calmly and quietly, especially if your child has oversensitive hearing. The child may try to withdraw or pull away to protect himself if the words are too loud.

2. Support the words with visual cues and gestures. Remember that permanent visual references always are available for later reference, and you can point to the picture, word, or object to remind your child of the direction. Visual references lead to independence from continually repeated verbal directions.

3. Speak naturally, but clearly, if you want the child to learn to understand the speech of others and if you want him to follow your directions.

    ♦ Use a normal tone and expressions. These gestalt learners with autism will learn and echo your tones and expressions without understanding when, where, and why those expressions are or are not appropriate.

Go shopping	
Yes Do	No, Can't Do
• Walk to store 　1. Bananas 　2. Crackers • Post Office • Home-lunch • Rules: 　1. Hold mom's hand 　2. Walk 　3. Talk softly	• Buy Candy? (crossed out) • Run? (crossed out) • Scream? (crossed out)

ILLUSTRATION 4. This T-chart prepares the child for a shopping trip.

- Speak at a normal rate. However, when introducing new information, slow the pace slightly, and pause at appropriate points for emphasis.

- Express a complete thought to clarify. For example, not "Let's go"; and not simply, "Get your coat on"; but, "Put your coat on. Then we will go to the park."

- Speak literally and specifically. For example, not "Sit down"; but, "Sit in the red chair." Not "Put the toys away"; but, "Pick up the toy trucks" (pause briefly), "and put them in this toy box." As you speak, model by picking up a toy and placing it in the box.

- Speak positively. Tell the child what to do. For example, not, "Don't hit!"; but, "Put your hands in your pockets." Not "Don't kick!"; but, "Keep your feet on the floor."

- Tell the child what he can and cannot do. This is a critical issue, because even if you tell him what to do, you cannot assume that he will not know what he cannot do. Provide visual reinforcement, such as that shown in Illustration 4.

4. Ask only important questions.

  ♦ Do not ask a question unless your child has an option. For example, the question, "Are you ready to eat now?" implies that there is a choice. If the child answers, "No" or does not respond, you can assume he means, "No." In that case, you cannot then coerce him to eat now. If you forget and ask such a question when there is no choice, regroup and say, "OK, I'll set the timer for 5 minutes. Then it will be time to eat."

  ♦ Avoid test questions. For example, questions such as, "What is this?" or "Is this red?" often are used for labeling pictures or to answer yes/no questions. There are several reasons to avoid these kinds of questions. The ability to label pictures or objects is a rote task that does not ensure an understanding of the object or the concept, nor does it guarantee that the child can use the word communicatively. In addition, test questions can result in a wrong answer. In that case, your child is likely to make a wrong association because he hears both the wrong answer and the right answer in relation with the object. For example, "No that's not red, that's blue." Finally, labeling tasks lack meaning and purpose. How many times in your life have you been asked a trick question ("Is this red?") or required to label pictures? Those with autism have too many things to learn to waste time on meaningless questions. There are many functional and meaning ways to determine whether a child understands a concept or word without using test questions.

5. Use contingency statements. A contingency is a contract that clarifies the work that must be completed before the payment is made (as in Grandma's rule, "First eat your peas. Then you can have ice cream"). Contingencies are powerful when used appropriately, for they provide information as well as motivation. Keep the contingency statement simple, clear, and positive. Negative statements

(e.g., "If you don't eat your dinner, you can't jump on the trampoline") do not motivate, and may trigger tantrums. It is more effective to say, "Eat your dinner. Then you can jump." There are at least three problems that typically occur with a negatively stated contingency.

- *Don't* statements are confusing. Most children with autism still will not know what to do. On the other hand, if the child does understand a don't statement, it literally sounds like, "You should not eat your dinner."
- When the child hears that he cannot do his favorite things, he falls apart. Perhaps part of the reason for this is that these very literal children may think, "Oh, no! I can't ever jump again."
- The amount of work is unclear. How much dinner will be required?

A positively stated contingency statement is more likely to motivate your child. An extra visual cue will signify the amount of work. For example, while you isolate five bites of food on the child's plate, say, "Eat *five bites*. Then you can jump on the trampoline." Another contingency is clarified in Illustration 5.

Contingencies not only improve motivation, they also are useful for teaching a variety of other critical concepts and skills that children with autism do not learn automatically. These include cause/effect relationships ("If this, then this"); sequencing ("First this, then this"); and trust in the adult who always pays off as promised.

6. Prepare your child for changes with visual information to support your words. Let the child watch as you draw and explain the changes. List any new rules, the activities that will occur, and any other information critical to the situation. A trip to the park is described in Illustration 6.

ILLUSTRATION 5. This visual aid clarifies a contingency statement.

ILLUSTRATION 6. This visual aid prepares the child for a trip to the park.

FINAL THOUGHTS

These simple strategies for giving clear directions and identifying and clarifying your child's needs will not only reduce his stress, but make life happier for you and your family. As you use these strategies you also are teaching your child to understand and use the language meaningfully.

As you read more about autism and teaching strategies, you may become confused; in one situation you are told to talk, but in another situation you are told not to talk. So, how do you proceed? There are some very basic guidelines. Naturally, you will talk when you are having fun and sharing experiences. You also will talk when introducing something new, when explaining changes, when providing feedback, and when your child's stress is at a low to moderate level (see Figure 10). But, there are indeed times when you stop talking—when your child's stress is high and when you are teaching him to perform a task independently. After you ask your child a question, pause to give him time to process the words. If we want our children to use the language, they must hear the language.

It is difficult to truly know when your child is attending to a conversation and to know how much of the language he understands. It is simply common sense to assume that if the child is present, he will understand (or perhaps misunderstand) at least some of the conversation; and it is common courtesy to include him in conversations, especially when he is the topic. For example, you can say, "Tommy, Aunt Betty wants to know what you like to do. Let's show her your play table."

It is gratifying to see your child's tense, uncomfortable little body relax when he begins to understand the language and when he knows exactly what to do. The worst thing we can do is to label a child's behavior from our perspective. When we decide that a behavior is an intentional and willful act of noncompliance or aggression, we do not look for the reason behind the behavior to identify the child's real problem and need. Without this understanding from the child's perspective, our interventions generally will make the situation worse.

These strategies are ones we use with friends, coworkers, and visitors from other cultures. The need is more pressing for children with autism. We can increase the time they can maintain equilibrium and spend productively when we understand autism and the kinds of situations that cause anxiety and when we give them the information they need in an understandable form.

STRATEGIES FOR ACHIEVING CRITICAL GOALS 10

Most young children are learning every minute of the day as they explore and experience their environment. It is almost impossible to keep them from learning. Children with autism also take in and remember information from the environment whenever they are alert; but all too often, they are withdrawn or tuned out, or they make incorrect associations and learn unexpected lessons.

For example, just as one child picked up a block, a door slammed. Startled, the child dropped the block and refused to touch it again. His mother, who was playing with him at the time, picked up the block and began to move it around. Touching him with the block, she said, "See? The block is OK. It was the door that made the loud noise. You can play with the block." As she continued to reassure him and play with the block herself, he began to do things with it. The child's gestalt processing style, which prevents analysis of information, had led him to associate the loud sound to his act of picking up the block.

A PERSPECTIVE OF TEACHING

Teaching new concepts and skills to those with autism is a challenging process. Their basic learning style results in quick, single-trial learning, but the bits and pieces or chunks of information they learn are filed in a fragmented form that cannot be flexibly or meaningfully retrieved and put back together for use. It takes both thoughtful planning and precise instruction to be sure that children with autism learn the complexities of concepts and skills and can generalize them to various situations. This type of planning and instruction is not difficult, but it does take time and practice to apply routinely.

This chapter contains a few examples of strategies for helping your child achieve the critical goals (see Figure 5). These examples may be enough to get you started at home, but in all cases you will need more detailed information and examples to get the most from the techniques.

GOALS AND INITIAL STRATEGIES

Most of the following suggestions integrate both cognitive and behavior strategies to ensure that your child will learn the intended lessons in a functional and meaningful way. You will note that each of the strategies addresses more than one goal.

Goal 1: To Value Interactions With People and Intentionally Initiate Communication

To learn:

- that people can provide information, assistance, pleasure, and comfort;
- to tolerate the closeness of people and to value social reinforcement;
- to play turn-taking games and initiate the actions of peers and adults;
- to intentionally seek out and spontaneously initiate interactions;
- to stay in interactions with people;
- to persist in efforts to communicate;
- to understand that people have a common, but different, experience or perspective; and
- to develop interdependent and cooperative relationships.

To help your child achieve these most critical goals, you will need to intrude yourself into his play and activities. Once you and your child begin this process, you both will have fun; in fact, fun is the critical element.

Strategy 1: Play Interactively With Your Child. Observe your child carefully before and as you play, to see what he does and how he responds to your stimulation. Your primary goal is to keep your child engaged—to keep him both intrigued and comfortable. If you stimulation exceeds his level of tolerance, he will withdraw.

This will be an intense interaction that requires the child's full attention. For the sessions to be successful, arrange an area that is fairly free of distractions (perhaps behind a couch, at the end of a hall, or behind a screen). Set up this relatively small area with only a few familiar and simple toys—a stuffed animal, a car or truck, a soft ball, or other favorites. At least initially, do not have any other children competing for your attention during the play session. Keep the session short—5–10 minutes, and gradually extend to 30 minutes when your child becomes more interactive and experimental. Try to schedule at least two or three play sessions each day.

- *Step 1.* Match your child's actions; that is, imitate. Do what he does (even if it is repetitive) with about the same intensity. When he stops, you stop and wait; then match his next action. Continue this routine for a while. Often during the first or second session, your child will suddenly discover what you are doing. He will stop and look directly at you, as if to say, "What are you doing?" Then the real fun begins as he starts to test you. He changes his routine slightly while watching you carefully, often from the corner of his eye, to see if he really can control your actions. This is the beginning of learning about the power of communication: "I do something, you do something."

- *Step 2.* Delay your imitation until your child stops to see whether you will follow. Then again imitate his actions. Now you are teaching your child to take turns, as in a conversation. Once he feels comfortable with this turn-taking routine, but before he loses interest and the routine becomes rote and repetitive, start the next step.

- *Step 3*. Imitate your child's actions, but add a subtle variation and wait for him to imitate you. Vary you speed, do the same action with a different object, or do a different action with the same object. Do not insist that he do what you do right then; simply offer the variation—a slight change of topic. Most likely, you child will watch you intently, but continue his original action; so, simply return to imitating his action. Throw in the same new topic periodically. When your child feels comfortable with it, he will try it. It is the subtle variations and the carefully timed pauses that keep his interest, maintain his tolerance, and expand his skills.

Notice that your child is in charge. You are making no demands except that he stay in the area. Talk or make noises only to match his sounds, words, and inflections. If he becomes overloaded with stimulation or demands, he will perceive you and your intrusions as painful and something to avoid; so remember that it is essential for both of you to have fun.

In the context of these pleasurable interactive play sessions, your child is developing a trusting and supportive relationship, which is the foundation for critical communication and social-emotional learning and other critical concepts and skills. Your child will make eye contact with you more often while he is learning:

- that he can initiate an interaction,
- that people are fun,
- to take turns,
- to maintain focus on the critical elements of an activity (you and your actions, and his actions),
- to increase attention and active involvement in an activity,
- to imitate the actions of other,
- to expand flexibility,

- to see that toys can be used in many different ways, and
- a myriad of other skills.

If your child's intervention program does not included these interactive play sessions, let his teachers know what you are doing, and collaborate in an effort to have them conduct these sessions at school as well.

If your older child with autism has not already learned these skills, this strategy can be modified to meet his needs. (For more information to expand and fine-tune these strategies, see Greenspan & Wieder, 1998.)

Strategy 2: Interrupt Your Child's Solitary Activities. Touch and talk to your child while providing personal care, and gently interrupt him when he is staring off into space, playing repetitively, or wandering randomly about.

- Move close to your child as he stares out the window. Touch his shoulder and say, "What do you see? I see the green leaves on the tree and a bird." Point as you say, "Look! A dog!" Pause. "Come, let's go into the kitchen. You can help make a snack." Gently but firmly guide him to the kitchen, and keep him involved near you by periodically showing him something or telling him to do some part of the activity (e.g., to hold, carry, rinse, fold).
- If your child is playing repetitively, sit in front or beside him and ask, "What are you doing? That looks like fun!" Then begin to imitate his actions for a minute or so, with variations as above. After several minutes, say something like, "Let's do this three more times. Then we can go outside and play ball."
- If your child is running and jumping from one thing to another, put your hand on his shoulder and say, "You need to run and jump. You run and jump in the (garage, playroom, outside)." Guide him to the appropriate area and, if possible, run or jump with him, or jump on a trampoline. Involve yourself with your child in some way. For example, take his hands as he jumps on a trampoline and when he

looks at you, say, "Jump!" If he looks away, say, "Stop!" as you stop his action. Continue to hold his hands, and when he looks at you again, say, "Jump!" or "Go!" and let him continue to jump. Expand the game to teach him to match his action to your words, "1-2-3-Go!" as he bounces for a while; then say "1-2-3-Stop!" Run races. Say, "Get ready! 1-2-3-Go!" and "1-2-3-Stop!" Perhaps you can take turns starting and stopping the activity. In this way, you are teaching your child to attend to you, listen for directions, follow a command, gain self-control, learn that there is a place to run and play, and learn that it is fun to do things with people. After several minutes of play, prepare your child for a clear ending to the activity. Say something like, "Three more times. Then it will be time to go in and play blocks." Remember that the goal is to keep him actively involved with people as much as possible. Note: I recognize that you cannot spend every moment with your child. The key is to play/work with him several times a day for 10 to 20 minutes each time, periodically interrupting his activity, joining the activity, and redirecting him to a more productive activity.

Goal 2: To Focus Attention on Critical Elements of the Environment and Maintain Active Involvement

To learn to:

- scan and focus on relevant information; to screen out and ignore irrelevant "background" information (sensory stimuli);
- watch others for information, shift focus from teacher to work, and match actions to actions of others;
- be actively engaged, sustain attention, to try, and to persist;
- sit at a desk or table and work independently in 1:1 sessions, and to participate meaningfully in small and large groups with others;
- work in different locations, with different adults and peers; and
- follow common classroom routines (e.g., take turns, stand or walk in line).

The strategies suggested above to achieve Goal 1 will address many of these Goal 2 skills as well, but they do not specifically address the need to teach your child to sit and work at a table. This is a critical, or pivotal, lifelong skill. I have been involved with older children who never learned to sit down and work at a table, either with a teacher or independently— children who never learned to sit at a table to eat. They simply floated randomly about the room, never centered, never engaged or productive. This situation becomes acute when these children grow physically larger, or when any demand or request for involvement or work triggers major tantrums.

Learning to sit and work at a table can begin as an extension of the interactive play strategies. Once the play sessions are running smoothly, you can add a new component.

Strategy 1: Transfer Materials From Floor to Table. Before beginning a play session, select two boxes or plastic dishpans. Label one *work* and the other one *finished.* In the work box, place one very simple, easy, and familiar toy—a simple puzzle, a shape box, or large pegs. If possible, arrange a small table near the play area. Place the finished box on the floor beside the table, to the child's right. As you and your child enter the play area, show him the work box, and say, "We will do this later." Then place the box off to the side. After playing for 10 minutes or so, give a warning that it is almost time to work. A few minutes later, indicate that it is time, and bring the box closer. Then say, "We can do this easier at the table." Pick up the box as you guide your child to sit at the table. Involve your child in taking out the work material and placing it on the table. Set the work box out of the way for now.

This placement of materials facilitates the concepts of working from left to right, taking out work, and putting it away when finished. These skills and concepts will be expanded later as the child learns to work independently.

ILLUSTRATION 7. This is an example of a mini-calendar. These small checklists clarify the number of tasks and the order in which they are to be accomplished within a short period of time.

On the first day, provide subtle assistance so your child finishes the task quickly. Place the toy in the finished box as you say, "You are finished. Time to play some more."

On succeeding days:

♦ Add variations. Vary the toys and the number of toys or activities included each day, and add new toys periodically. These variations help to maintain motivation, increase the time the child can sit and work, and increase his flexibility as he adjusts to new materials.

♦ Prepare a mini-calendar—a checklist of the tasks to do each session. (See Illustration 7.) Show your child how to draw a line through the task as it is finished.

Strategy 2: Develop Routines and Rituals to Help Your Child Focus on Work and Prepare for Transitions. Mark the beginning and end of an activity with a ritual that involves taking materials out and putting them away. A ritual can be attached to the use of a simple calendar that lists the activities of the day. For example, your child will pick up a symbol (an object or a picture) that represents *time to brush teeth*. The child carries the symbol to the bathroom and brushes his teeth, and when he is finished, he takes the symbol back to the calendar and places it in a container (a box or an envelope) labeled *finished*.

There are other strategies and motivation issues to consider as you expand the work and play sessions to increase your child's ability to attend and engage in productive activity.

Goal 3. To Learn the Language and Communicate Effectively

To learn:

+ that everyone has a label (sometimes multiple labels);
+ that some words have multiple meanings;
+ that context changes meanings;
+ that words, toys, and pictures are symbols for real things;
+ that words can be spoken and written down and have meaning;
+ that objects and actions have a purpose that can be labeled;
+ that words can label and define concepts and relationships;
+ the power of words and communication to send clear messages;
+ to imitate the sounds and actions of others;
+ to use gestures, objects, and words to communicate meaningfully;
+ to understand the language spoken by others; and
+ the meaning of verbal directions and rules, and to respond independently (e.g., "Get ready"; "First work, then play"; "Point to ___"; "Give me ___"; "Come here").

Children with autism need to *hear* the language in order to *understand and use* the language. Our tendency is to stop talking or to talk in very stilted ways, because these children do not give us much feedback and we know they have trouble processing the words they hear. The strategies for teaching and giving directions (see pp. 153–157) will help your child achieve some of these goals, but we also must provide a good model of the language.

Strategy 1: Talk to Your Child. Use "Parallel Talking." When you are working beside or caring for your child, carry on a running commentary that labels the things you are using and doing. It is much like that of the radio sports announcer, who explains the players' actions so that someone who is not present can tell what is happening. It is different in that you speak naturally, but you keep the language simple and clear. Incorporate pauses at the ends of phrases to give you child time to process the information.

- Do not ask questions or make demands. Answering questions and following directions will be addressed at a different time. The purpose of this type of parallel talking is to give the child an accurate model of the language in natural contexts—the labels of things, descriptive words, and so on.
- Point to or in some way highlight or connect the object and the label. While putting your child's shoes on, say, "Your shoe is untied." (Tap or squeeze the shoe and flip the shoestring.) "First, I pick up the string and pull it tight." (Pull with slightly exaggerated movements.) "Now, I cross the strings." (Again, match your words with exaggerated moments.) Continue to explain as you tie the shoe.

In your commentary, include words that describe the colors, sizes, shapes, and the parts of objects (the parts of a toy or a game). Use gestures to pair the spoken label with the object.

Strategy 2. Draw Pictures of Things and Events. Capitalize on your child's visual strengths and great memory to teach language. I found that my students with autism were fascinated and watched intently when I made line drawings or wrote words to clarify expectations as I talked, so I kept a pencil and small pad in my pocket at all times to be ready to clarify a situation.

Your child needs to know that there are *real* things, and *pictures* of those things.

- When you have been playing together with a small toy (say, a dinosaur), lay it on a card or piece of paper and trace around it with a black marker while your child watches. As you draw, say, "This is a picture of the dinosaur." (Pause) As you add a very few details, say, "This is the dinosaur's eye, . . . and this is its mouth . . ." Hold it up and say, "See? This is a *picture* of the toy dinosaur," (then hold up the toy) "and this is the toy dinosaur." Name each letter as you print the label. Then point to the word, and say, "this is the *word* dinosaur." If you use 3" x 5" cards, you can keep them in a small file box to review periodically. You also can use them to sort and categorize ("The pictures of animals go here, . . . and all of the pictures of things we eat go here").

- After you have finished an activity with your child, draw a very simple picture of your activity. For example, one day Tommy and I were sitting in front of a mirror. I called his attention to our reflections while we rolled a big ball back and forth between us. When we finished playing, I quickly drew a picture of our activity. As I drew the picture, I described what I was doing. "This is a picture of Tommy. T-O-M-M-Y." (Pause) "This is a picture of Jan. J-A-N." (Pause) "This is a picture of the ball. B-A-L-L." As I held up the picture and pointed to each figure, I said, "This is a picture of Tommy and Jan rolling the ball, and these are our names."

When you draw, use a simple stick figure form, free of cute or extraneous details. These simple illustrations highlight only the critical elements of the environment and are quick to draw.

Strategy 3: Place Labels on Objects and Areas. Each day, spend a few minutes labeling different things in the house. On one day, label different kinds of windows, and on another day, label different kinds of chairs. Make labels on white 3" x 5" cards, using a black marking pen or crayon. Join the ends of a short piece of masking tape to make a roll with the sticky part outside. Place the role of tape on the back of the card, and press the card on the object. With your child at your side, place your hand on a mirror, and say, "This is a mirror." With a 3" x 5" card placed so your child can watch, print *mirror* as you say each letter and the word ("M-I-R-R-O-R. This is the word mirror.") Place the roll of tape on the back of the card, hand the card to your child, say, "Put the word mirror on the mirror," and help him to do it quickly. Then say, "Let's find another mirror," and repeat the procedure. It is important for the child to see that the bathroom mirror, a hand mirror, and the mirror in the hall are all different, but they have the same name. Use the same or similar strategy to teach your child the label of any newly acquired toys, furniture, or other objects.

Strategy 4. Take Advantage of Every Opportunity to Help Your Child Communicate. If your child is not yet verbal, and you know he wants something, prompt him to use his communication system by saying, "You can show me what you want." If the child wants a cookie, guide his finger to point to a cookie or the picture of the cookie as you say the words, "You want a cookie," or "Want cookie." Pause briefly in case he attempts to say the word. Then give the cookie. Take advantage of every possible situation to allow him to practice—to learn the power of communication. The strongest reinforcer for learning to communicate is to get the things he wants as a natural result of his own actions.

Many parents fear that if their child is taught to use gestures, signs, or pictures to communicate, he will never learn to talk. This just is not so. We now know that verbal communication often begins to develop once a child learns to communicate in whatever way is easiest. We also know that simply learning to verbally label pictures and objects is no guarantee that those words will be used to communicate intentionally. To actually use words to communicate meaningfully depends on an understanding of the power of communication.

Goal 4: To Tolerate Change and Accept New Experiences; to Be More Flexible

To learn:

* that materials, schedules, and settings can be used and arranged flexibly;
* that there are alternative ways and times to do things; and
* that change is OK, and new things can be interesting.

Strategy 1: Develop and Maintain a Basic Routine of Events That Occur Each Day. A daily schedule is the second most valuable behavior management tool. Only the communication system is more important. Children with autism will be more relaxed and comfortable with change and new activities if they occur in the context of familiar routines. Generally, there are enough interruptions at home to provide some variations; but if there are not, make a point of changing at least one thing every day.

* Set up a daily calendar—a visual structure—to help your child manage those changes. Use a chalkboard (or white board) on a wall, a sheet of paper, or a chart with 3" x 5" cards. Place the calendar at his eye level. List the main events of the day in order, without too much detail. The activities of the day can be represented by real objects, line drawings, or printed words, depending on your child's needs. (See Illustration 8.)
* Review the calendar with your child each morning. Touch the symbol, and say the name of each activity as you proceed down the list. Your child learns to tolerate changes in his schedule because he is reassured by the familiar schedule and the fact that most things will remain the same. Teach your child to mark off the symbol for each activity as it is completed. In this way, the calendar will help your child measure the passing of time and prepare for coming events. Soon you may

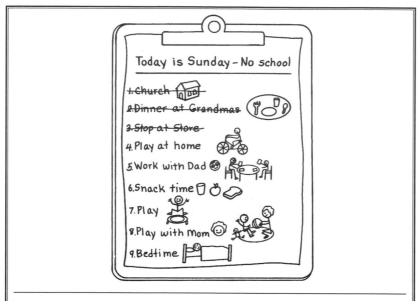

ILLUSTRATION 8. This is another example of a daily calendar. Each morning, write a list of the day's events on a chalkboard or a piece of paper. Explain the events to your child as you write.

see your child go to the calendar independently to check on the next activity. He may even try to rearrange the day's schedule by eliminating the symbols for activities he dislikes. When your child begins to do these things, you will know that he understands and really uses the daily calendar.

There are many different ways to develop and use schedules and calendars to match your child's changing needs. Some children need to use real objects instead of pictures or written words to represent activities; the objects are set up in a sequence of trays. Other children have their calendars set up in notebooks. You will want to work with your child's teacher and use similar strategies at home and at school. If the same type of schedule is used in both settings, your child's life will be much less stressful and he can be more flexible.

Goal 5: To Do Things Independently Without Constant Verbal Direction

To learn:

♦ to follow visual information systems (schedules, calendars, and work systems), and

♦ functional work and self-help routines for doing purposeful things.

The strategies described above also apply to achieving this goal. As your child learns to use calendars, checklists, and cue cards, he will become even more independent.

Strategy 1: Teach Self-Help Skills in the Context of Complete Routines. You now know that those with autism learn and use skills exactly as taught, so if we want them to do something independently, we much teach it that way from the very beginning.

Because it is relatively easy for children with autism to learn routines and they generally like to repeat familiar routines, we teach basic self-help skills in the context of routines. For your child to be able to manage his basic life activities independently, he must be taught all of the steps involved in the routine, from the beginning of the routine to the end. Not only does he need to learn when, where, and how to do the routine, but if he is to be totally independent, he also must learn how to solve problems, get help, and end the routine. (See the brief example of the tooth-brushing routine, pp. 104–105.)

Once you learn to design and teach functional routines, you can use the technique to teach your child many different routines—an eating routine, a bedtime routine, and a routine for feeding the cat or going to the store. The process for developing and teaching these functional routines is not hard, but it does involve a number of steps and more information than can be included in this space.

Strategy 2: Stop Talking When You Reach a Routine That Your Child Ultimately Is to Do Independently. Verbal directions and prompts are almost impossible to eliminate. These one-trial learners repeat routines exactly as taught, forever. If you continue to talk and give the same verbal directions after about the second day of instruction, your child will expect that you always will be a part of the routine ("First, Mom says, 'Do ___.'" Then I ___. Then Mom says, 'Do ___,'" and so on). When we try to fade out of the routine and stop giving the directions, the child will wait—and wait, and wait—for us to take our turn. Finally, in frustration we give the direction, and the child follows it. That is how we build such strong dependence on verbal directions. You can avoid this problem.

1. As you plan the routine, develop a visual checklist (using pictures or words) that includes all of the steps.

2. On the first day, as you introduce and teach the routine:
   - Show your child the checklist, and quickly point to and describe each step.
   - Demonstrate the routine, highlighting each step on the checklist as you proceed. As you demonstrate the routine, use the parallel talk strategy (see p. 170) to provide the language for each step.

3. On succeeding days:
   - Review the checklist with your child before beginning the routine.
   - Then reduce your talking and increase the use of gestures, pointing, and touching prompts to refer your child to the checklist and keep him moving fluently through the routine.

4. Within a few days:
   - Stop talking, and use only the necessary prompts to prevent errors.

Goal 6: To Develop Self-Monitoring and Self-Management Skills

To learn:

* to identify stressful feelings;
* to ask for and take a break;
* to relax, and then to reengage in the ongoing activity;
* to accept correction;
* to ask for assistance, make choices, and identify and solve problems; and
* to develop a self-control routine.

Yes, children with autism can learn to monitor their stress and their behavior, and they can learn self-control routines to calm themselves and remain productive. Some can use these skills independently, while others can do the skills with reminders.

Strategy 1: Teach Your Child to Recognize His Own Feelings. Your child needs to pair the language of feelings with his own feelings. This occurs when you:

* recognize his behavior signals of stress, excitement, confusion, and other feelings;
* acknowledge his feelings; and
* help him to resolve the problems that trigger those feelings (see p. 151).

Strategy 2: Teach Your Child to Ask for and Take a Break. This involves identifying the things or situations that are relaxing to your child, and arranging a location for taking a break. One preschool child was taught to give a signal to the teacher when she needed a break. Then she ran to the back of the room and rocked in a small rocking chair. After rocking vigorously for several minutes, she began to relax, and finally, she returned independently to participate in the group. This process was taught in the context of a routine (as described on p. 91).

Strategy 3: Systematically Teach Your Child Relaxation and Visualization Strategies. At the Groden Center (http://www.grodencenter.org), children begin to learn progressive muscle relaxation when they first enter the program. It is best to begin teaching these skills as soon as possible. Although the teaching process is not hard to learn, you will need detailed information and perhaps some specific training before you begin to ensure that your child will become independent.

FINAL THOUGHTS

Parents and teachers must work together to ensure that the child with autism will become as independent as possible. Neither the parents nor the teachers can do it alone. Most of the strategies are easy to implement at home in the context of your family's natural routines and activities, but it does take time and practice to use them effectively.

It is important for you to remember that development does not occur in a smooth, linear fashion. For any child, there are spurts of growth; periods of reorganization when a child's behavior fluctuates between calm and irritable; and times when there is no evidence of new skills. There also are periods of regression, during which the child seems to go back to a much younger age and lose skills. This is a particularly disheartening period for parents of children with autism. If you can maintain your equilibrium and avoid too much discouragement, if you can press calmly on, maintaining your schedules and calendars and collaboration with teachers, your child will have spurts of growth and become ever more independent.

PART V
THE GIFTS

THE GIFTS OF AUTISM ![11]

While writing this book, I read *The Gift of Dyslexia*, by Ron Davis (1994). It is not often that such a positive book is written about any of the various learning differences. Davis honored those with the "gift" of dyslexia as he suggested that their intuitive way of thinking is the foundation of genius. His intervention approach involves people with compassion providing appropriate teaching methods to help these children learn literacy skills while maintaining and supporting their gifts. You may be interested in the fact that as a child, Davis had received a diagnosis of autism and dyslexia.

Individuals with autism also have gifts. The gifts of autism occur as a result of their strong visual abilities, attention to minute details, unusual interests, and amazing memory. Other common traits, such as honesty, naiveté, gentleness, compliance, and perfectionism, are exceedingly refreshing and unexpected in this increasingly cynical world. Some of the children seem to automatically excel at certain skills. The ability to focus intensely on the unexpected and the literal, the concrete understanding of the language and the environment, leads to "enchanting logic," as expressed by Bill Seaton (see the haiku on p. 185).

The gifts of those with autism are commonly in the fields of music, mathematics, poetry, the visual arts, history, and trivia. These strengths and interests often lead to acceptance, respect, friendships, and interesting occupations, hobbies, and leisure activities.

INTENSE INTERESTS
PROVIDE MOTIVATION

Intense interests or fixations of a few individuals have led to opportunities for advanced study and recognition beyond family and community, as in the case of Temple Grandin. As a child, Temple suffered terribly from overwhelming stimulation, and frequently she was tense and painfully anxious. There seemed no way to help her relax. While visiting her aunt's cattle ranch, Temple noticed that when nervous cattle were put in the cattle press to receive their shots, they relaxed immediately. The change in the cattle's behavior as they were in the press made a deep impression on Temple. She wanted to see whether the feeling of the pressure on her own body would help her relax. After considerable pestering, her aunt placed her in the press. The pressure felt so relaxing to Temple that she wanted her own cattle press at home. This fixation continued until her science teacher, working with her parents, gave her the challenge to find out why the pressure helped her and the animals to relax.

That was the beginning of her study of animal psychology and her career as a college professor and designer of humane cattle-handling facilities for meat packing companies and ranchers. Temple also designed and sold her own squeeze machine (see Gerlach, 1996). But, that is not all; she has achieved international acclaim for her work in human animal treatment and in autism (Grandin & Scariano, 1989).

The importance of capitalizing on the learning strengths and interests common to those with autism is mentioned throughout this book. Many individuals are intensely interested in some very specific types of objects or activities. The abilities of others are not as easy to identify, and not every fixation results in worldwide acclaim; but many have resulted in more productive and interesting lives.

- One little girl could spend hours spinning about without ever getting dizzy. Although this looked strange in many places, her mother decided that it would look very natural on ice. After instruction, the girl became a very good skater who excelled in spins. Ice skating provided the opportunity for the physical release she craved, so she no longer needed to spin when she was off the ice. Skating was an excellent lifelong recreational and leisure skill that brought recognition and friendships.

- Another child became fascinated (obsessed) with light bulbs. Each and every light bulb caught and held his attention. His family supported this interest and helped him organize his growing collection of bulbs. As he grew older, he began to correspond with office managers who worked in different light bulb manufacturing companies. They sent him catalogs, price lists, and other information. When I saw him last as a teenager, he was responsible for cleaning and maintaining the light fixtures in an office building.

- A man with autism, who is a very orderly perfectionist, was employed in the office of a large hospital. It was his job to keep all hospital files in the correct order. Soon after starting this job, he began to find the hospital's lost files. When I asked him how he could be so good at this job, he replied, "It's just natural-born talent." And so it is.

- One of my former students had an intense interest in TV schedules. By the time he was 5 or 6 years old, he had the schedules memorized. If asked when a certain program could be viewed, he knew the time, the channel, and the cast of characters. He also enjoyed watching TV programs about history, nature, and other real events, and he remembered the dates and facts. As a young adult, he participated in a national trivia tournament that was broadcast to local bars across the country. In fact, for a while he was the national champion of this trivia event. Not only did he gain a great deal of respect from others, but he truly enjoyed the evenings at the bar with friends.

- As a child, Burleigh was fixated on shredding every paper in sight. After many unsuccessful intervention efforts to eliminate the behavior, his mother finally got control over all of the papers in the house and set aside some that she gave him every now and then as a payment (reinforcer) for a period of hard work or, at other times, to help him relax. As

Burleigh grew older, he shredded cardboard. Now, as an adult, he owns his own paper shredder and has contracts with a number of businesses to shred the confidential records of previous clients. This young man with severe autism is nonverbal and has a "friend" to provide assistance as he travels to the various job sites. His father, Bill Seaton, wrote:

As Burleigh was growing up, it was hard for me to understand why he did so many of the things he did. Like, when he was 8 or 9 years old, he might pour out my day's supply of coffee just as I was putting on my coat to go to work—something that would just put me into a rage. . . . At times, it reminded me of my high school days of learning to play basketball. There were days when it almost would seem that I had somehow gotten "wrong footed" by Burleigh.

At other times, I would find myself marveling at little things, like how artfully Burleigh would hand me a plate or a cup—the precision in the way he handed me things. He would not let go until my hand made contact to grasp it. It reminded me of getting a good baton pass in a relay race. Even the strange things that he does are done with amazing deftness. When he puts torn cardboard into a garbage can, it is tightly packed, like a beaver constructs a dam.

I still haven't been able to see just what is going on with him, but I have confidence now that there is a rhyme and reason to it. . . .

A haiku first poses a mental image of something, and then it twists that picture to some degree. It struck me that I frequently found myself having that experience with Burleigh. I would be looking at some random behavior of his, and then be startled to realize that it had a depth of decision behind it. That was the feeling I tried to express with this haiku:

Autism shrouded mind
Acting out bizarre, belies
Enchanting logic.

ARTISTS WITH AUTISM

Although there are many artists with autism, three have been featured in the autism literature. These artists display and sell their work at autism conferences and art shows. Jesse Parks, who lives in Massachusetts, makes amazingly detailed drawings of buildings, among other things. A British artist, Richard Wawroe, creates naturalistic and highly detailed scenes of British life and the countryside. Mark Rimland, who lives in San Diego, CA, paints exceptional watercolors. Mark illustrated the children's book, *The Secret Night World of Cats* (Landalf & Rimland, 1998).

Four Leaf Press (Eugene, OR) publishes and sells greeting cards featuring artists with autism. Two of their artists have allowed me to share some of their drawings.

*   Rosemarie Williams, from Pennsylvania, was 5 years old in 1994 when she was diagnosed with autism. These pictures were drawn at about that time (see Illustrations 9 and 10). Her mother, Karen Williams, wrote:

> She began drawing before she could communicate with words. Rosemarie still draws all the time, sometimes drawing very well, other times drawing very simply, and a lot of times the drawings are repetitive. But they all have much meaning to her, and she loves them all. Rosemarie draws a unicorn whose name is Annalee (you will recognize her in the drawings). This is Rosemarie's alter ego, and everything that happens to Rosemarie happens to Annalee. It is a very important way for Rosemarie to process information.

ILLUSTRATION 9. Running With the Wind, by Rosemarie Williams.

ILLUSTRATION 10. Annalee and Friends, by Rosemarie Williams.

◆ Kim Miller, of Roseburg, OR, was 2 years old when her autism was diagnosed. Before she was comfortable looking at faces, she began drawing them on the bottom of her bare toes. She began to speak

ILLUSTRATION 11. Your Hand in Mine, by Kim Miller.

Kim's mother told me that from birth, Kim was highly sensitive to touch. At the time Kim drew this picture at age 5, she was unable to hold anyone's hand and walk calmly. Her mother said, "It touches my heart, because she chose to take the walk with me."

when she was almost 5 years old. By the time she was 6, she was drawing three-dimensional pictures. Although she has never had art lessons, she can draw in many different styles. Sometimes she begins a drawing with a seemingly insignificant element in the middle of the page (e.g., the bow on the back of the girl's dress in Illustration 11), and she draws lines out from that point to complete the picture. At other times, she begins by drawing the figures from the background out to the foreground. Occasionally, she starts with a line as if it were the top of a silhouette, and then works down. Her mother says that she draws quickly,

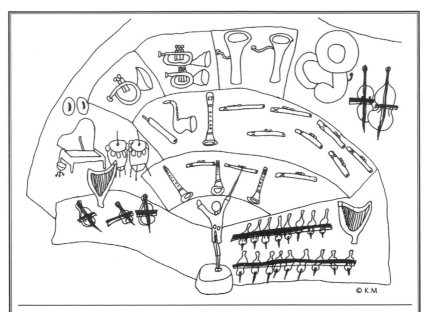

© K.M.

ILLUSTRATION 12. I Hear a Symphony, by Kim Miller.

Kim drew this picture when she was in a music class in second grade. She had always been incredibly sensitive to sound, but once she learned that the instruments made certain sounds, she became fascinated and even obsessed with music and musical instruments.

It is noteworthy that there is only one person in this drawing—and we don't see his face. Is this an illustration of the theory that those with autism are not hot-wired to attend to faces?

not pausing or hesitating to contemplate her next move. Within a matter of a minute or less, she would have the full picture completed without making a mistake, with all intersecting lines perfectly aligned, and often in three dimensions. You could tell, by watching how she was so precise and confident, that she already had the picture in her mind, just how it would be [see Illustration 12].

As Kim draws she cannot keep her body still. Her father says, "The paper stays in place, but her body moves all around it." She draws just as well upside down, sideways, or diagonally. If something truly pleases her, she jumps up, bounding and flapping, and then settles down to the paper again. When very young, Kim would draw 50 or more pictures a day. Now, at age 10 ½, she has become more social and involved, and generally she draws only when she is excited or feeling upset.

POETS WITH AUTISM

It seems amazing that individuals with such pervasive language and communication disorders would be able to write poetry, but some do. The poetry reprinted here has much to tell us about how it feels to have autism.

♦ Nick Gerlach is 12 years old. His mother wrote:

He has autism, and is fully mainstreamed in school with the help of an assistant. He enjoys playing percussion in the sixth grade band. He wrote this poem during the first few weeks of hand practice in response to his teacher asking if he heard the beat. Nick has enjoyed drumming since the third grade, when he performed solo on bass drums in a school performance. He has expressed interest in playing timpani in a symphony some-day. Always musical, Nick also likes to sing (with near perfect pitch). Interestingly, Nick will sometimes put his most sincere thoughts into the form of a song and sing them instead of speak them. Perhaps it is easier for him to communicate certain feelings this way.

Nick began to write poetry last spring. This is his latest poem.

I Hear the Beat

The beat is in my head.
Always in my head.
People talk, I hear the beat.
Machines go, I hear the beat.
Lights are on, I hear the beat.

People walk, I hear the beat.
Always, always hear the beat.

In school, they say,
Stop the beat, and do your math.
Stop the beat, and write.
Stop the beat, and listen to my words.

Can't stop the beat.
It's in my head.
Always, always hear the beat.

In band now he says,
Hear the beat?
Of course, of course
I hear the beat.

♦ In 1985, I read a small book of poems titled *UNDERSTAND: Fifty Memowriter Poems*, written by David Eastham. David could not write or speak and was unable to express his thoughts until he learned to communicate on a small computer when he was 19 years old. The eloquence of David's poetry convinced me that one must be continually aware that there is a sensitive person inside everyone with autism, and that the limit of any person's potential is never certain. David's plea to "UNDERSTAND" represents what I hope to accomplish in this book. (For David's life story and more poetry, read *Silent Words* and *Forever Friends*, by Margaret Eastham and David Eastham [1990a, 1990b].)

HYPER PEOPLE
HYPER PEOPLE TRY
TOO HARD,
TRY, CRY, SIGH
I THINK UNLESS THEY STOP
I'LL DIE, DIE, DIE

YOU ARE SO CALM
YOU UNDERSTAND
YOU WANT ME TO
BE A MAN

HAPPY FEELINGS
TODAY I FEEL
HAPPY
TEACH ME JOKE
TEACH MY LOVE
AND GREATNESS
TEACH ME FUN
AND TEACH ME
SOME
OF EVERYTHING
YOU
POSSESS

KISS WITH EYES
KISS WITH EYES THEY DO
I SEE IT ALL THE TIME
GOD I ENVY PEOPLE
KISSING WITH EYES
THE LOVE FLOWS LIKE
STARS LIKE BRILLIANT
STARS
SO REALLY LOVING HOW
I LOVE TO KISS WITH EYES

UNDERSTAND
I WANT PEOPLE TO
    UNDERSTAND
I KNOW ITS HARD TO DO
I THINK THEY CAN, IF
    THEY TRY
UNDERSTAND WON'T YOU?
UNDERSTANDING IS SO
    HARD
I LONG TO SEE IT REAL
I JUST HOPE, REALLY HOPE
IT'S NOT A LOST IDEAL

GLOSSARY

analytic processing—an information-processing style. Information is taken in, processed, and analyzed for meaning, then stored for easy recall, flexible use, and expansion.

applied behavior analysis (ABA)—a research procedure used by behaviorists to study behavior change; to study the effects of different ways to manipulate the cues, prompts, and consequences to teach new behaviors or to weaken or eliminate ineffective behavior. In the past, this systematic process of behavior change was known as *behavior modification*.

augmentative communication—methods for supporting communication. When unable to reliably communicate verbally in the traditional way, a person is taught to use other ways to support or augment communication. Augmentative (or alternative) communication systems include pictures, electronic devices, signing, and gestures.

behavior—any observable activity. Behavior change is defined as an observable and measurable change in behavior activity.

behavioral approach—a teaching approach based on the theory that behavior can be studied accurately through the analysis of an individual's response to the environment. Behavior strategies are those that manipulate the environmental cues, prompts, and consequences to encourage learning.

behavior management—the processes and procedures to be used to prevent behavior problems, to manage problem behaviors that do occur, and to prevent the problems from recurring. These procedures are generally spelled out in a behavior management plan. Classroom teachers have a plan to maintain appropriate student behavior. A plan will be developed for an individual child who has severe behavior problems so that all involved in the child's program will know what to do.

behavior modification—another term for applied behavior analysis.

cognitive—pertains to the mental processes of thinking, knowing, and reasoning.

cognitive/developmental approach—a teaching approach based on the theory that behavior is influenced by environmental conditions and by what one believes to be true about the environment. It also considers that a child's belief system depends on mastering a predictable sequence of developmental states. Cognitive strategies are those that provide information to clarify meaning and prevent false beliefs, and that encourage thinking and reasoning.

consequence—an event that occurs as a direct result of a response; that is, a reaction to the response. The type of consequence will influence the strength of a response and determine whether the same response is likely to recur or be modified. There are three basic types of consequences: reinforcement, punishment, and correction procedures.

contingency—a contract that specifies and clarifies expectations. It defines the expected behavior (the work or effort) and the reinforcement (the payoff). Contingencies often are stated in the when/then format that provides motivation.

correction procedure—a response to an error or incorrect response that occurs in the process of instruction. A correction procedure directs the learner back to the original cue and provides another chance to make a correct response and receive a reinforcer. For example, if a child is asked to get his red sweater, but brings his blue one instead, you would take the blue sweater without any comment about the error; and while it is out of the child's view, say, "You need your red sweater." Go quietly with the child, and as you point to the red sweater, say, "Get your red sweater."

critical goals—those goals that compensate for the deficits of autism.

cue—a signal or situation that stimulates or triggers a response. For example, a stop sign is a cue or signal that triggers me to stop my car. Other terms that are sometimes used with the same meaning are *antecedent*, *stimulus*, or *event*.

discrete trial—a distinct and finely defined teaching unit most often associated with the Intensive Behavioral Intervention model. Each discrete trial involves: (1) the teacher presents a cue; (2) the child responds; (3) the teacher delivers the reinforcer; and (4) there is a brief pause. Then the same task is prepared for a set number of times (massed or repeated trials). The trials (opportunities to respond) can be scheduled in several different ways.

echolalia—the repetition of speech produced by others. The echoed words or phrases can include the same words and exact inflections as originally heard, or they may be slightly modified.

floortime—an application of the interactive play strategies developed by Greenspan and Wieder.

functional—useful; practical. Functional goals lead directly to greater independence in the real world, such as eating, dressing, doing laundry, and managing a bank account. Functional routines are a set or sequence of steps or procedures directed to achievement of a practical purpose; for example, all of the steps involved in washing dishes, from knowing when to wash dishes all the way to having clean dishes in the cupboard.

generalize—to learn to use a skill that was taught in one situation, and then use it in other situations. For example, a child learns to say, "Hi!" to his teacher at school. The skill is generalized when he learns to say, "Hi!" to his mother, a friend in the hall, or his friend at the store. The child has overgeneralized the skill when he says, "Hi!" to his teacher every time he looks at her all day long, or he says it to everyone he meets on the street whether he knows the person or not.

gestalt processing—the distinct information-processing mode common to those with autism. Information is taken in, recorded, and stored quickly in whole units, or "chunks," without analysis for meaning.

incidental teaching format—a procedure for setting up or engineering opportunities for the child to practice skills in natural situations. For example, the teacher stands between the child and the cookie (blocks access), and as the child reaches for the cookie, the teacher shapes his reaching hand to a point and speaks for the child, "Want that cookie," and quickly gives him the cookie. This format allows a teacher to take advantage of teachable moments that occur when the child spontaneously indicates a need.

information-processing approach—the study of the sensory systems (auditory, visual, and so on) and the processes that are involved in learning—the study of how information is taken in from the environment, processed, and used.

integrated approach—a teaching approach that incorporates the knowledge and principles from the four different approaches to the study of learning: the neurophysiological, information-processing, cognitive/developmental, and behavior approaches.

Intensive Behavioral Intervention (IBI)—refers to an intensive treatment model based on the principles of ABA. In this context, intensive implies 1:1 instruction for many hours every day over an extended period of time. The model makes use of the discrete trial instructional format. IBI generally is used in reference to the intensive early intervention model developed at UCLA by Lovaas.

interactive play strategies—strategies that are an application of the incidental reaching format that calls for the adults to be less directive and dominating and allows the child to take the lead. In fact, the adult follows the child's lead in play. These highly effective strategies address the profound social and communication deficits common to those with autism.

interpreter—one who can explain, clarify, or provide the meaning of events, words, and experiences; one who guides and provides assistance to reach a goal; one who highlights important details, attracts the eye, and provides quick reference.

learning theory—the study of how learning occurs and the resulting ideas and principles that explain learning.

neurophysiological approach—the study of the development of the brain structures, including the central nervous system, and the interactive effects of that development on learning; that is, learning stimulates more complex brain development, which in turn stimulates more advanced learning.

perseverate—the redundant repetition of words, thoughts, or motor movements without the ability to stop or move on.

pivotal skills—highly specific skills or responses that are critical to successfully participate in many different situations or tasks. For example, learning to respond, learning to request, and learning to persist are pivot skills. Pivotal response training involves a modification of the ABA principles. It depends on the incidental teaching format to teach and generalize pivotal skills in natural situations.

prompt—something added or assistance provided immediately after a cue to ensure a correct response (to prevent an error). For example, if I am daydreaming at the checkout stand and don't respond to the natural cue (the total due that appears on the screen), the checker will put out his hand, palm up, to prompt me to pay.

reinforce—to strengthen or to increase the strength. A reinforcer is something pleasant and valued that occurs (or is received) as a consequence of a response. A response that is reinforced is likely to be repeated or strengthened.

response—a behavior or action that occurs as the result of a cue. For example, when the baby cries (the cue), I provide a bottle (the response).

sensory systems—the neurological pathways and processes for receiving, processing, and integrating information from the environment. The systems include the sensory channels (e.g., the eyes—the visual channel; the ears—the auditory channel).

structured teacher—a systematic process developed at the TEACCH program, for visually organizing and structuring the environment, so the child always knows exactly what to do, when and where to do it, and how to do it. The visual structure reduces anxiety, highlights critical information, and allows the child to become increasingly independent.

syndrome—a condition characterized by a cluster of co-occurring symptoms that has a specific effect on a group of individuals; for example, fetal alcohol syndrome, Down syndrome, autism.

REFERENCES

American Psychiatric Association. (2000). *Diagnostic and statistical manual of mental disorders* (4th ed., text rev.). Washington, DC: Author.

Biederman, G. B., Fairhall, J. L., Raven, K. A., & Davey, V. A. (1998). Verbal prompting, hand-over-hand instruction, and passive observation in teaching children with developmental disabilities. *Exceptional Children, 64,* 503–511.

Birnbrauer, J. S., & Leach, D. J. (1993). The Murdoch early intervention program after two years. *Behavior Change, 10*(2), 63–74.

Bondy, A., & Frost, L., (1998). The picture exchange communication system. *Advocate, 30*(5), 7–9.

Boutot, E. A. (2009a). Using naturalistic instruction for children with autism. In E. A. Boutot & M. Tincani (Eds.), *Autism encyclopedia: The complete guide to autism spectrum disorders* (pp. 275–280). Waco, TX: Prufrock Press.

Boutot, E. A. (2009b). What are autism spectrum disorders? In E. A. Boutot & M. Tincani (Eds.), *Autism encyclopedia: The complete guide to autism spectrum disorders* (pp. 21–26). Waco, TX: Prufrock Press.

Church, C. C., & Coplan, J. (1995). The high-functioning autistic experience: Birth to preteen years. *Journal of Pediatric Health Care, 9,* 22–29.

Cohen, H., Amerine-Dickens, M., & Smith, T. (2006). Early intensive behavioral treatment: Replication of the UCLA model in a community setting. *Journal of Developmental & Behavioral Pediatrics, 27,* 145–155.

Crozier, S. (2009). Social stories. In E. A. Boutot & M. Tincani (Eds.), *Autism encyclopedia: The complete guide to autism spectrum disorders* (pp. 231–235). Waco, TX: Prufrock Press.

Davis, R. (1994). *The gift of dyslexia.* Burlingame, CA: Ability Workshop Press.

Dawson, G., & Osterling, J. (1997). Early intervention in autism: Effectiveness and common elements of current approaches. In M. J. Guralnick (Ed.), *The effectiveness of early intervention: Second generation research* (pp. 307–326). Baltimore: Paul H. Brookes.

Donnellan, A. M. (1984). The criterion of the least dangerous assumption. *Behavioral Disorders, 9,* 141–150.

Eastham, D. W. (1985). *UNDERSTAND: Fifty memowriter poems.* Ottawa, Ontario, Canada: Oliver-Pate.

Eastham, M., & Eastham, D. W. (1990a). *Forever friends.* Ottawa, Ontario, Canada: Oliver-Pate.

Eastham, M., & Eastham, D. W. (1990b). *Silent words.* Ottawa, Ontario, Canada: Oliver-Pate.

Education for All Handicapped Children Act of 1975, Pub. Law 94-142 (November 29, 1975).

Frith, U. (1989). *Autism: Explaining the enigma.* Oxford, UK: Blackwell.

Frost, L., & Bondy, A. (2002). *Picture exchange communication system training manual* (2nd ed.). Newark, DE: Pyramid Educational Products.

Gerlach, E. K. (1996). *Autism treatment guide.* Eugene, OR: Four Leaf Press.

Gerlach, E. K. (1998, January). Beetlejuice therapy and other treatments for autism. *The Net: Newsletter of the AUTISM Society of Oregon, 7.*

Grandin, T. (2006). *Thinking in pictures: My life with autism* (Expanded ed.). New York: Vintage Books.

Grandin, T., & Scariano, M. (1989). *Emergence: Labeled autistic.* Novato, CA: Arena Press.

Greenspan, S. I., & Wieder, S. (with Simons, R.). (1998). *The child with special needs: Encouraging intellectual and emotional growth.* Reading, MA: Addison-Wesley.

Groden, J., & LeVasseur, P. (1995). *Cognitive picture rehearsal: A system to teach self-control.* In K. A. Quill (Ed.), *Teaching children with autism: Strategies to enhance communication and socialization* (pp. 287–305). New York: Delmar.

Hamilton, L. M. (2000). *Facing autism: Giving parents reasons for hope and guidance for help.* Colorado Springs, CO: Waterbrook Press.

Hart, C. (1989). *Without reason: A family copes with two generations of autism.* New York: Signet Books.

Individuals with Disabilities Education Act, 20 U.S.C. §1401 et seq. (1990).

Janzen, J. E. (1998). *Understanding the nature of autism: A practical guide*. San Antonio, TX: The Psychological Corporation.

Klinger, L. G., & Dawson, G. (1992). Facilitating early social and communicative development in children with autism. In S. F. Warren & J. Reichle (Eds.), *Volume 1: Causes and effects in communication and language intervention* (pp. 157–186). Baltimore: Paul H. Brookes.

Koegel, R. L., & Kogel, L. K. (Eds.). (1996). *Teaching children with autism: Strategies for initiating positive interactions and improving learner opportunities*. Baltimore: Paul H. Brookes.

Landalf, H., & Rimland, M. (1998). *The secret night world of cats*. Lyme, NH: Smith and Kraus.

Lovaas, O. I. (1987). Behavioral treatment and normal educational and intellectual functioning in young autistic children. *Journal of Consulting and Clinical Psychology, 55,* 3–9.

Rimland, B. (1995). Editor's notebook: Is there an autism epidemic? *Autism Research Review International, 9*(2), 3.

Rogers, S. (1996). Brief report: Early intervention in autism. *Journal of Autism and Developmental Disorders, 26,* 243–246.

Sallows, G. O., & Graupner, T. D. (2005). Intensive behavioral treatment for children with autism: Four-year outcome and predictors. *American Journal on Mental Retardation, 110,* 417–438.

Schopler, E., Van Bourgondien, M. E., & Briscol, M. M. (1993). *Preschool issues in autism*. New York: Plenum Press.

Strain, P. S., & Cordisco, L. K. (1994). LEAP preschool. In S. L. Harris & J. S. Handleman (Eds.), *Preschool education programs for children with autism* (pp. 225–252). Austin, TX: Pro-Ed.

Tincani, M., & Groeling, S. (2009). Introduction: Emerging issues in causes, assessment, and intervention. In E. A. Boutot & M. Tincani (Eds.), *Autism encyclopedia: A complete guide to autism spectrum disorders* (pp. 1–10). Waco, TX: Prufrock Press.

Venn, M. L., Wolery, M., & Greco, M. (1996). Effects of every day and every other day instruction. *Focus on Autism and Other Developmental Disabilities, 11,* 15–28.

Wetherby, A., & Prizant, B. (1999). Facilitating language and communication development in autism: Assessment and intervention guidelines. In D. B. Zager (Ed.), *Autism: Identification, education, and treatment* (2nd ed., pp. 107–134). Hillsdale, NJ: Erlbaum.

Wing, L. (1980). Foreword. In C. Webster, M. Konstantareas, J. Oxman, & J. E. Mack (Eds.), *Autism: New directions in research and education.* Elmsford, NY: Pergamon Press.

Wolery, M., Bailey, D. B., & Sugai, G. M. (1988). *Effective teaching strategies: Principles and procedures with exceptional students.* Boston: Allyn & Bacon.

ABOUT THE AUTHOR

J anice E. Janzen was challenged to learn about the unique autism learning style when a child with autism was enrolled in her class in 1972. Since then, she has taught children with autism; provided training and consultation services to teachers and parents; developed and implemented Oregon's Regional Autism Services model; written technical assistance and training materials and special topics papers; and conducted autism workshops across the country.